How To Know
the Father's Voice

by
Bill Basansky

Harrison House
Tulsa, Oklahoma

Unless otherwise indicated, all Scripture references are taken from the *King James Version* of the Bible.

Some Scripture quotations marked AMP are taken from *The Amplified Bible, Old Testament*. Copyright © 1965, 1987 by Zondervan Publishing House, Grand Rapids, Michigan. Used by permission.

How To Know the Father's Voice
Revised
Previous Library of Congress
  Catalog Number: 78-57651
ISBN 0-89274-888-5
Copyright © 1992 by Bill Basansky
Bill Basansky Ministries
P. O. Box 7126
Fort Myers, Florida 33911

Published by Harrison House, Inc.
P. O. Box 35035
Tulsa, Oklahoma 74153

Contents

Preface

Matthew 3:16,17 says:

And Jesus, when he was baptized, went up straightway out of the water: and, lo, the heavens were opened unto him, and he saw the Spirit of God descending like a dove, and lighting upon him:

And lo a voice from heaven, saying, This is my beloved Son, in whom I am well pleased.

This example of Jesus is still plain for all to follow as they are led by the Spirit to know the Father's voice through the pages of God's Word.

Yet today, as in the days of Christ's earthly ministry, many fail to hear what the Father says. Like those referred to in John chapter 12, their ears are tuned to the wrong message. Jesus prayed:

Father, glorify thy name. Then came there a voice from heaven, saying, I have both glorified it, and will glorify it again.

The people therefore, that stood by, and heard it, said that it thundered: others said, An angel spake to him . . . .

John 12:28,29

The people of that day are just like the people of today! Some are like those who heard the "thunder" — they insist on being very "scientific" and "intellectual" in their approach to God's Word, explaining its accompanying miracles as only "phenomena of nature." In the other extreme, people become "super-spiritual" — listening to personal prophecies, looking for "angels," or for signs.

Between the two extremes is the Truth that *God speaks*. And His voice comes to glorify the name of Jesus, saying **I have both glorified it, and will glorify it** *again* (John 12:28). That's the reason I have written this book. It is my prayer that it will help you to be led by the Spirit and *glorify* the name of Jesus — *again* and *again* and *again* — as you learn to *know the Father's voice!*

———————————

————

"You must start right where you are and trust God to guide you, personally."

————

———————————

1

Start From Where You Are

Many Christians have expressed to me their sincere desire to know the voice of God. They want to be led by the Holy Spirit. Yet, in the same breath they say, "But I don't want to make a mistake or be led by the wrong spirit. There's a storm in my life; I'm afraid, so I hesitate. I don't know when and how to start."

We can only start from where we are. If we fear the storm and postpone our journey until it's over, we may never begin. Therefore, I suggest that you start learning to be led by God's Spirit right now — storm or no storm.

> He who observes the wind [and waits for all conditions to be favorable] will not sow, and he who regards the clouds will not reap.
>
> As you know not what is the way of the wind or how the spirit comes to the bones in the womb of a pregnant woman, even so you know not the work of God Who does all.
>
> In the morning sow your seed, and in the evening withhold not your hand; for you know not which shall prosper, this or that, or whether both alike will be good.
>
> **Ecclesiastes 11:4-6** AMP

In order to plot your course, you must have proper charts. You must know where you are going and try to go there the best possible way.

We must begin with several basic truths, truths that we must have settled in our spirits about God. As Christians, we should have a revelation knowledge of Jesus Christ that will determine our course throughout life.

1. We must know that God has spoken to man. The Bible — His Word — gives us power and wisdom unto salvation.

2. We must know that Jesus Christ is Lord and King over all His world. He rules all things for His own glory, displaying His perfections in all that He does in order that men and angels may worship and adore Him.

3. We must know that Jesus Christ is our Savior and His love is sovereign to rescue believers from darkness, from guilt, and from the power of sin. He adopts us into the family of God as His sons and blesses us accordingly.

4. We must know that God is triune and that within the Godhead there are three persons: Father, Son, and Holy Spirit. In the work of salvation, all three persons of the Godhead act in harmony: the Father purposing redemption (John 3:16,17), the Son securing it (Eph. 1:7), and the Holy Spirit applying it (Eph. 1:13, John 16:13).

5. We must also know that "godliness" simply means responding to God's revelation and turning to Him in trust and obedience, in faith and worship, in prayer and praise, in submission and service.

The life of Christ can only be seen in our lives as we live according to His teachings. The Holy Spirit never leads a believer apart from God's Word. Therefore, it is essential that every believer study the Scriptures. (2 Tim. 2:15.)

God's Ways Are Revealed in His Word

As we study God's Word with receptive hearts, we begin to see what pleases Him, what offends Him, what awakens His wrath, what affords Him satisfaction and joy. (Prov. 6:16-23.) As we seek to do His will, God reveals Himself to us through His Word by the precious Holy Spirit. Thus, our spirits (regenerated by Christ) will be in tune to the revelation of the Spirit, and we will know and understand the voice of our heavenly Father.

Many Christians have expressed that they have problems walking in faith and in being guided by the Spirit of God. That is not because they *doubt* that divine guidance is a fact, but because they are *sure* that it is. I'll explain.

They know that God can guide and that He has promised to guide every believer. Yet, because they have listened to others relate personal experiences, these Christians who seek His will begin to fear they will fall short of such experiences for themselves. Therefore, they become afraid that they will miss God's guidance through some fault or weakness of their own. They seem to have no doubt that God guides others, but they remain uncertain of their own receptivity to His guidance. Thus, they just sit, refusing to move, becoming frustrated and tormented by the devil.

Again, may I encourage you not to look at the storm. If you postpone your journey until the storm subsides, you may never learn to be led by God's Spirit. Romans 8:14 says, **For as many as are led by the Spirit of God, they are the sons of God.**

You must start right where you are and trust God to guide *you*, personally. Begin now to develop your confidence in the fact that *God is totally good*, that **Every good gift and every perfect gift is from above, and cometh down from the Father . . .** (James 1:17). Look up and begin to thank Him for His willingness and ability to protect you, to teach you and to do nothing but good things in your life. The Holy Spirit will show you the way.

Remember this: God's will will never *lead* you where He cannot *keep* you.

———————

———

"As you read His Word, train your spirit to listen for what He says to you, personally. As you do this, you will become tuned to God's voice in ways far beyond natural comprehension."

———

———————

2
God Has a Perfect Plan for You

Most people who aren't being led by the Holy Spirit seem to be grouped into one or more of the following categories:

1. They are not sure of their position with their heavenly Father.

2. They have not sincerely desired from God the guidance they need.

3. They are not sure that God is willing to work in their lives.

4. They are not sure that God has a plan for their lives.

5. They aren't convinced that God will communicate with them personally.

God Has Always Had a Plan

God had a plan for the deliverance of His people from Egyptian bondage when he led them through the Red Sea and through the desert with a pillar of cloud by day and a pillar of fire by night. He was well able to take care of them, protect them, and direct them.

God had a plan for Jesus. (Luke 18:31.) Jesus' whole ministry on earth was to do His Father's will (John 4:34), and He accomplished His mission (Matt. 1:21; Eph. 1:7).

God had a plan for Paul. (Acts 21:14; 22:14; 26:16-19.) In many of his letters, Paul announced himself as an apostle ''by the will of God.''

God has a perfect plan for each of His children. He has a plan for *you,* and He is able to communicate His plan to *you,* personally.

Detailed Accounts of Divine Guidance

The Bible contains many accounts of how God guided His people and revealed His plans to mankind. The book of Acts includes several instances where detailed guidance is described:

1. Philip being sent to a desert place to meet the Ethiopian eunuch. (Acts 8:26-39.)

2. Peter being told to accept the invitation of Cornelius. (Acts 10:19.)

3. The church at Antioch being charged to send Paul and Barnabas on a mission. (Acts 13:2.)

4. Paul and Silas being called into Europe. (Acts 16:6-10.)

5. Paul being instructed to press on with his Corinthian ministry. (Acts 18:9.)

We see in these accounts that guidance may come in dreams, visions and through direct, verbally given messages. Yet, *all of these must be judged and verified with the Word of God by the Holy Spirit's witness with our spirits and by the peace that comes within our own hearts.*

The Bible is filled with examples such as these from the book of Acts. However, these are sufficient to make the point that God has no difficulty in revealing His will to those who seek Him in earnest.

Since He is no respecter of persons (Acts 10:34; Rom. 2:11), what He did for believers in New Testament days, He will do for *you!*

Divine Guidance Is Also for Today

The Scriptures contain explicit promises of divine guidance. Through these promises, we may know God's plan for our lives today, and we may know His will regarding each course of action that we take.

Psalm 32:8 says:

> **I will instruct thee and teach thee in the way which thou shalt go: I will guide thee with mine eye.**

Isaiah 58:11 gives full assurance that when people repent of any wrong-doing in their lives and instead obey the Lord, He will guide them continually:

> **And the Lord shall guide thee continually, and satisfy thy soul in drought, and make fat thy bones: and thou shalt be like a watered garden, and like a spring of water, whose waters fail not.**

In Proverbs 3:6, we read:

> **In all thy ways acknowledge him, and he shall direct thy paths.**

David prays for protection and guidance in Psalm 25:8,9,10a, saying:

> **Good and upright is the Lord: therefore will he teach sinners in the way.**
>
> **The meek will he guide in judgment: and the meek will he teach his way.**
>
> **All the paths of the Lord are mercy and truth . . . .**

In Colossians 1:9, Paul prays for the Christians to be filled with the knowledge of God's will . . . **in all wisdom and spiritual understanding.**

He encourages them to **be strong in the Lord, and in the power of his might** (Eph. 6:10), and to **stand perfect and complete in all the will of God** (Col. 4:12).

Here, it clearly states that God is always ready to make His will known. Wisdom in the Scriptures means knowledge of what action pleases God and secures life. He promises in James 1:5 that:

> **If any of you lack wisdom, let him ask of God, that giveth to all men liberally, and upbraideth not; and it shall be given him.**

According to Paul, when believers present themselves to God in "reasonable service" and refuse to "conform to the world" in their lifestyle, it brings a complete transformation of character:

> **I beseech you therefore, brethren, by the mercies of God, that ye present your bodies a living sacrifice, holy, acceptable unto God, which is your reasonable service. And be not conformed to this world: but be ye transformed by the renewing of your mind.**
> **Romans 12:1,2a**

Paul says when we do this, we *prove* **what is that good, and acceptable, and perfect,** *will of God* (v. 2b).

The Bible contains many other truths that give full assurance that God will guide His people:

> **The steps of a good man are ordered by the Lord: and he delighteth in his way. Though he fall, he shall not be utterly cast down: for the Lord upholdeth him with his hand.**
> **Psalm 37:23-25**

> **A man's heart deviseth his way: but the Lord directeth his steps.**
> **Proverbs 16:9**

For thou has, delivered my soul from death: wilt not thou deliver my feet from falling, that I may walk before God in the light of the living?

Psalm 56:13

He maketh me to lie down in green pastures: he leadeth me beside the still waters.

Psalm 23:2

For this God is our God for ever and ever: he will be our guide even unto death.

Psalm 48:14

The meek will he guide in judgment: and the meek will he teach his way.

Psalm 25:9

Howbeit when he, the Spirit of truth, is come, he will guide you into all truth ....

John 16:13

You Are Chosen

Always remember that Christian believers are chosen by the Lord Himself. They are called "sons of God." If human parents have the responsibility of giving their children guidance in cases where ignorance and incapacity mean danger, we should not doubt that *God is infinitely more concerned for us.* He says in Matthew 7:11:

If ye . . . know how to give good gifts unto your children, *how much more* shall your Father which is in heaven give *good things* to them that ask him?

It seems that people easily recognize the voice of the devil. Why not begin to recognize the voice of God? Who is your Father? Don't you know His voice? Certainly you do! For Jesus said in John 10:4,5:

> . . . he putteth forth his own sheep, he goeth
> before them, and the sheep follow him: for they know
> his voice.
>
> And a stranger will they not follow, but will flee
> from him: for they know not the voice of strangers.

(In verse 14, He declares Himself to be the Good
Shepherd.) (Also, see John 10:1-30.)

To be led by the Spirit, you must be sensitive to
God's voice. You become sensitive to what He says
only as you allow His Word to have its rightful place
in your day-by-day life. As you read His Word, train
your spirit to listen for what He says to *you*, personally.
As you do this, you will become tuned to God's voice
in ways far beyond natural comprehension.

Some time ago during a seminar, reservations
were made for me at one of the older motels in that
town. When I checked in, the clerk showed me where
I was to stay. It was a nice room, with plenty of space.
Yet, there was an inner voice that told me not to stay
there.

I said, "No, this isn't the room: do you have
another one?"

Finally, I was shown a very small room with one
of the windows cracked. It didn't look very good, but
God's voice within me said, "This is the one."

The clerk couldn't understand why I chose the
small room. In the natural, the first one was much
better. It wasn't cramped, and it was more inviting.

That night, two men checked into the room I had
turned down. They were to leave early for an
appointment. But the next morning when the maid
knocked on the door and opened it, both men were

dead. There was a leak in the open-flame gas heater. It was not detectable by smell. What happened to those men was tragic. No one could have known that it would happen, and that tragic event could have happened to me. Yet, because I was sensitive and obedient to the Holy Spirit's leading, my life was saved. I was sensitive because I have a daily habit of reading God's Word.

Get To Know God's Word

You will see more of God's plan for your life unfold as you realize that:

> All scripture is given by inspiration of God, and is profitable for doctrine, for reproof, for correction, for instruction in righteousness:
>
> That the man of God may be perfect, thoroughly furnished unto all good works.
>
> 2 Timothy 3:16

Jesus has given us the Holy Spirit to help us understand God's Word. He dwells in us as our Comforter, Teacher, and Guide. Jesus said:

> If ye love me, keep my commandments.
>
> And I will pray the Father, and he shall give you another Comforter, that he may abide with you for ever;
>
> Even the Spirit of truth; whom the world cannot receive, because it seeth him not, neither knoweth him: but ye know him; for he dwelleth with you, and shall be in you.
>
> But the Comforter, which is the Holy Ghost, whom the Father will send in my name, he shall teach you all things, and bring all things to your remembrance, whatsoever I have said unto you.
>
> John 14:15,16,17,26

Before we can expect the Holy Spirit to do His work and bring the words of Jesus to our *remembrance,* we must first be acquainted with what He has said. We do this by reading the Scriptures.

I feel compelled to point out here that Christian books, regardless of their content, will never take the place of His words. The sermons that Jesus preached, the teachings that He gave, the words that He spoke, can never be equalled. And if you haven't read what *He* says to *you* through the Gospels, I suggest that you take advantage of every opportunity to read these four inspired accounts of the greatest Life ever lived! Your own life will take on richer meaning and God's plan for *you* will be made real.

―――――――

―――――

*"As you prepare your life for God's
guidance, realize that the Holy Spirit has
but one mission on earth —
to exalt Jesus and to make Him more
real to believers. He doesn't come
to promote any particular creed or
doctrine, any individual layman or church
personality. He doesn't even come to
exalt Himself. His only ministry is
to lift up Jesus and to see people drawn
to Him in worship and adoration."*

―――――

―――――――

3

How To Prepare
for God's Guidance

From the Scriptures that I have already given, no one reading this book should ever again doubt that divine guidance is promised, that it is for today, and that it is given to every child of God.

Christians who miss God's guidance or direction show only that they did not seek it as they should. Therefore, you should be concerned about your own receptivity to His guidance and study His Word to seek to be led by His Spirit. *You should begin now to educate your spirit and train yourself to be sensitive and receptive to the voice of God.*

You should not only be convinced of God's *will* to guide you, but you should also *prepare yourself for God's guidance.* You must keep your heart pure — for out of it are the issues of life. (Prov. 4:23.)

The psalmist David said:

> **If I regard iniquity in my heart, the Lord will not hear me.**
>
> **Psalm 66:18**

If we willfully sin and refuse to honor God in our lives and are not worshipping and praising Him as Lord, we cannot expect His guidance:

> **Now we know that God heareth not sinners: but if any man be a worshipper of God, and doeth his will, him he heareth.**
>
> **John 9:31**

On the other hand, when we obey God's Word and seek to *do* what is right in His sight, we can expect Him to lead us and to answer our prayers continually:

> **Beloved, if our heart condemn us not, then have we confidence toward God.**
>
> **And whatsoever we ask, we receive of him, because we keep his commandments, and do those things that are pleasing in *his* sight.**
>
> **1 John 3:21,22**

If God does not hear your prayer, then you can't possibly hear from Him and receive His guidance. But when you live a godly life and He is *glorified* in you, Jesus said:

> **Whatsoever ye shall ask in my name, that will I do, that the Father may be glorified in the Son.**
>
> **If ye shall ask any thing in my name, I will do it.**
>
> **John 14:13,14**

In Psalm 23:3b, David declared that God gives guidance for His own honor and glory:

> **He leadeth me in the paths of righteousness for his name's sake.**

God's Word becomes a lamp for our lives, and the light for our path:

> **Thy word is a lamp unto my feet, and a light unto my path.**
>
> **Psalm 119:105**

Walk in the Light of God's Word

Often Christians who seek God's guidance go about it in the wrong way. They do so because their spiritual senses are out of focus. They only look for an emotional experience, an inward prompting. They overlook the guidance that has been right there beside them all along — *the Word of God.*

In failing to see the value of the Scriptures in guiding their lives and shaping their destinies, these people leave themselves open to all sorts of delusions. Their basic mistake is to think of guidance as essentially an *inward prompting by the Holy Spirit, apart from the written Word.*

This idea is as old as the false prophets in the Old Testament. It is a bad seed from which all forms of fanaticism can grown. It will always mislead you, causing you to err from the truth.

Many Christians make this mistake and are being led away from the truth because of a personal need or problem. They listen to other people or read books and testimonies of those who say, "God led me or God told me." Because they cultivate a desire for such experiences in their own lives without preparing themselves through the knowledge of God's Word, they plunge headlong into the depths of destruction:

My people are destroyed for lack of knowledge.
Hosea 4:6a

Admittedly, there are personal needs that are very real. I have deep compassion for people who hurt, and in my spirit I hurt with them and want to see their needs met. Yet, we must never take the short-cuts that nullify God's laws of deliverance which He reveals in the Bible.

It is imperative that you be fully convinced of the Holy Spirit's leading in your personal life and not base your actions upon someone else's leading or emotions.

One example of what I mean can be found in John 11:1-46. In this passage, Jesus purposely delayed His visit to the home of Lazarus. Although His friends and followers wanted Him to hurry because Lazarus was sick unto death, Jesus took His time. He arrived later than everyone expected, yet the biblical account of Jesus raising Lazarus from the dead reveals that, regardless of how it appeared to others, Jesus was *right on time* with God!

You must let *faith* and *compassion* be your rule rather than presumption and sympathy or any other human emotion.

Learn To Trust God's Timing

One time when I was in California, I had just come home from a hard day of activity. A Christian lady called me: "Will you go and pray for my husband who is very sick in the U.C.L.A. hospital?"

The man had several incurable diseases, and the doctor had already pronounced his case hopeless.

"No," I said, "I can't go." I didn't feel any witness from the Lord that I should go at that time.

Friends condemned me. They didn't understand. They thought my heart was calloused and my spirit not sensitive to the real need.

I went to prayer: "Lord, I want to go, but not just because someone tells me to go." Still, I did not have the craving within me to go pray for the man.

All the time, the man's condition grew worse. He had an enlarged heart, a fever of 105 degrees, and lips that were swollen so large they cracked. Every time the machine pumped blood, it would ooze through the cracks in his lips.

Early one morning, after a week of fervent prayer, the Lord gave me a vision of the man. I saw him rise from his bed, totally healed.

The Holy Spirit told me, "Go to the hospital now and pray for him." I called the man's wife and told her I was on my way.

By the time I got to the hospital, the hospital staff had virtually given up because of this man's poor condition.

I prayed for the man, in Jesus' name. He was completely restored, *and he was saved!* The doctors and nurses all admitted that it was a miracle of God, and his wife rejoiced in his salvation, too.

The Lord said, "See — if you had gone before it was My time for you to go, I would have received no glory, and he would have died unprepared."

In my vision, I had also seen flowers, and I told the man's wife, "God will receive him home later, but He will first heal him and *save* him." He lived a beautiful life after that, but not as a sick man. When he later went on to heaven, his family was comforted in the fact that he was ready to meet God.

Again, I emphasize to you that God never leads us or causes us to take any action that is contrary to His Word. You must read the Word of God for yourself, knowing that it is His revelation to *you*, personally.

Know also that God has given to the church the ministries of capable pastors, evangelists and teachers to help His people know His Word more clearly:

> **And he gave some, apostles; and some, prophets; and some, evangelists; and some, pastors and teachers;**
>
> **For the perfecting of the saints . . . .**
> **Ephesians 4:11,12**

Paul told Timothy:

> **And the things that thou hast heard of me among many witnesses, the same commit thou to faithful men, who shall be able to teach others also.**
> **2 Timothy 2:2**

A Word of Caution

It is good to listen to men who are anointed of God and energized by the Holy Spirit. It is good to read their books and other faith-building materials. In doing this, you will:

> **Study to shew thyself approved unto God, a workman that needeth not to be ashamed, rightly dividing the word of truth.**
> **2 Timothy 2:15**

Yet, know also that you must not listen to every whim and doctrine, for the next verse in that chapter says:

> **But shun profane and vain babblings: for they will increase unto more ungodliness.**
>
> **2 Timothy 2:16**

While you have the responsibility to *listen* to the *truth* that you may grow in your Christian life, you are also admonished to *reject error.*

How do you accomplish this? Realize and be willing to face the cold fact that everyone who professes to have truth is not in the *Truth.* Of such, John said:

> **They went out from us, but they were not of us ....**
>
> **1 John 2:19**

He continues:

> **I have not written unto you because ye know not the truth, but because ye know it . . . .**
>
> **1 John 2:21**

Then, knowing that Truth is stronger than error and that the Spirit of Truth will cause the believer to triumph, John says with full confidence:

> **These things have I written unto you concerning them that seduce you.**
>
> **But the anointing which ye have received of him abideth in you, and ye need not that any man teach you: but as the same anointing teacheth you . . . ye shall abide in him.**
>
> **1 John 2:26,27**

It's very important that you see the connection of these verses I gave you in First John, chapter two. In the statement, **ye need not that any man teach you** (v. 27), John isn't referring to the gifted teachers God has placed in the church (Eph. 4:11). He is referring directly to those men who "went out from us" (v. 19), the false

31

teachers who deliberately try to "seduce" (v. 26) or mislead believers from the truth.

To Lift Up Jesus Is the Goal

As you prepare your life for God's guidance, realize that the Holy Spirit has but *one* mission on earth. It is to exalt *Jesus* and to make Him more real to believers. He doesn't come to promote any particular creed or doctrine, any individual layman or church personality. He doesn't even come to exalt Himself. His only ministry is to lift up Jesus and to see people drawn to Him in worship and adoration. Christ promised:

> **Howbeit when he, the Spirit of truth, is come, he will guide you into all truth: for he shall not speak of himself . . .**
>
> **He shall glorify me: for he shall receive of mine, and shall show it unto you.**
>
> **John 16:13,14**

You must acknowledge, too, that the Holy Spirit is a *Person* — the third *Person* of the Trinity. Thus, He has a *personality* of His own and must express Himself as He pleases. It's imperative that you see this and that your own personality always be in submission to *His personal expression.*

There will be times when He wishes you to be meek and retiring; other times He may want you to be bold and forward. At times, He may want you to remain silent and at other times to be quick to speak out. But know this: if your motive is to lift up Jesus and see Him glorified among men, you are at *one* with the Spirit. *If this is your aim, you are prepared for His guidance, and you can be certain of His full cooperation!*

———————

———

*"I caution you to not get
religion — all in your head — without letting
Jesus grow in your heart. It's possible
to formulate a religion out of Christian
dogma by memorizing Scripture verses,
yet never see Jesus in a revelation
of truth."*

———

———————

4
How To Walk With Jesus

Of the things we have covered thus far about educating our spirits, this is the sum:

1. To learn how to be guided by the Holy Spirit, you can only begin from where you are, and the best time to begin is *now*.

2. You should be confident that God has a plan for your life and believe Him to guide you into its fulfillment.

3. You should prepare yourself for God's guidance:

   a. Accept the Bible, God's Word, as His supreme revelation to man.

   b. Have confidence that the Holy Spirit will lead you, personally.

   c. Submit yourself to the ministry gifts that God has placed in the church for your edification and Christian growth.

   d. Cooperate with the Holy Spirit in His *one* mission on earth, *exalting Jesus among men.*

Now that you are prepared for God's guidance and are on your way to receiving it, *don't get religion — get Jesus.* By this I mean, don't let experiences and Christian dogma become your lifestyle; rather, let your thoughts and conduct center on the person of Jesus Christ and seek to exalt Him in all you do and say.

It's possible for Christians to develop the same attitude toward Jesus that the Old Testament Israelites had toward the manna. (Ex. 16.) When God sent down the miraculous bread from heaven, they were cautioned by Moses that they should gather a sufficient amount for each day and believe God for each day's needs. But the Bible says:

> **Notwithstanding they hearkened not unto Moses; but some of them left of it until the morning, and it bred worms, and stank . . . .**
>
> **Exodus 16:20**

In like manner, it's possible for your Christian experience to become out-dated, powerless, and without effect. *But your life in Christ can be ever new and fresh as you educate your spirit to live it one day at a time!* You can believe Him for new experiences each day that you live, for . . .

> **Jesus Christ [is] the same yesterday, and to day, and for ever.**
>
> **Hebrews 13:8**

He is the Bread of Life who was sent down from heaven to satisfy the hunger of all who believe.

Jesus said to the people of His day, and He says to *you:*

> **. . . Verily, verily, I say unto you, Moses gave you not that bread from heaven; but my Father giveth you the true bread from heaven.**
>
> **For the bread of God is he which cometh down from heaven, and giveth life unto the world.**

**. . . I am the bread of life: and he that cometh
to me shall never hunger; and he that believeth on
me shall never thirst.**

John 6:32,33,35

He Gave Them "Manna"

It's interesting to note that the word *manna* means
what is it?

On the day it fell from heaven, the Israelites saw
it and didn't know what to call it, so they said:
"Manna" which means "What is it?"

Forty years later, they were still eating it, and they
still didn't know, nor did any of the new generation
know, what it was.

**And he humbled thee, and suffered thee to
hunger, and fed thee with manna, which thou
knewest not, neither did thy fathers know . . .**

Deuteronomy 8:3a

Why?

**. . . that he might make thee know that man doth
not live by bread only, but by every word that
proceedeth out of the mouth of the Lord doth man
live.**

Deuteronomy 8:3b

This should tell you the value that God places
upon His Word and emphasize the vital part it should
have in your life.

The miracle of the manna, as great as it was, still
had its basis in the Word of God. In fact, all miracles
today must have their basis in God's Word.

For this reason, the writer of Hebrews asks:

> **How shall we escape, if we neglect so great salvation; which at the first began *to be spoken* by the Lord, and was confirmed unto us by them that heard him;**
>
> **God also bearing them witness, both with signs and wonders, and with divers miracles, and gifts of the Holy Ghost . . . .**
>
> **Hebrews 2:3,4**

"Manna" — "What Is It?"

Not until Jesus stood there in their midst and made His astonishing proclamation that He is the **bread of life** (John 6:35) that **came down from heaven** (John 6:38), did the people of Israel have the Answer to that question. And even then, some of them never really *knew.* They heard Him say it, but they still couldn't *see* it.

On the Day of Pentecost when the Holy Spirit was poured out, people came into contact with the miraculous and saw signs and wonders confirming God's Word, but they still asked, **What meaneth this?** (Acts 2:12) — "What is it?" Today, it is no different. They come and see, but they still ask, "What meaneth this?"

On the Day of Pentecost, Peter gave the answer. Beginning with the Prophet Joel and continuing through Bible history to the crucifixion and resurrection, Peter preached unto them *Jesus.* (Acts 2.)

"What is it?"

The Answer is *Jesus!*

Jesus is the Answer!

Jesus Is the Answer!

He is what this whole thing is about. He is why the move of the Holy Spirit is sweeping across the world today. *Jesus* is being exalted among all people!

When I emphasize the value of God's Word, I mean the revelation of Truth that's made real to you by the Holy Spirit. I'm talking about *heart knowledge,* not mere mental assent. Jesus said:

> **The words that I speak unto you, they are spirit, and they are life.**
>
> **John 6:63b**

That's why I caution you not to get religion in your head without letting Jesus grow in your heart. It's possible to formulate a religion out of Christian dogma by memorizing Scripture verses yet never see Jesus in a revelation of Truth.

This is how the scribes and Pharisees treated the Old Testament Scriptures. They memorized great passages and could quote them at length. Yet, they did all things in the form of their *religious traditions.* Jesus told them:

> **Thus have ye made the commandment of God of none effect by your tradition . . . well did Isaiah prophesy of you, saying, This people draweth nigh unto me with their mouth, and honoreth me with their lips; but their heart is far from me.**
>
> **Matthew 15:6b-8**

The religious leaders of Jesus' day had an illness that is widespread among many religious people today — an inflation of the head but a deflation of the heart. They made a commitment to the Scriptures, but not to *Jesus.* They never saw Jesus in the Word, so they could never believe on Him with their hearts and be saved.

To these religious leaders, Jesus said:

> **And ye have not his [God's] word abiding in you: for whom he hath sent, him ye believe not. Search the scriptures; for in them ye think ye have eternal life: and they are they which testify of me . . . . had ye believed Moses, ye would have believed me: for he wrote of me. But if ye believe not his writings, how shall ye believe my words?**
>
> **John 5:38,39,46,47**

You Must See Jesus

As you seek God's guidance, the Holy Spirit will always lead you to the Word. There, with the Holy Spirit's enlightenment, you will see Jesus — from the first chapter of Genesis where all things were spoken into existence by the Word (John 1:1-14) until the final prayer in Revelation 22:20 which says, . . . **even so, come, Lord Jesus**.

By educating your spirit to *walk with Jesus,* you will develop the attitude of the late Billie Sunday who wrote this *Tribute to the Bible:*

> Many years ago, with the Holy Spirit as my guide, I entered the wonderful temple of Christianity. I entered the portico of Genesis, walked down through the Old Testament Art Galleries, where pictures of Noah, Abraham, Moses, Isaac, Jacob and Daniel hung on the wall.
>
> I passed into the music room of Psalms, where the Spirit swept the Keyboard of

Nature until it seemed that every pipe and reed in God's organ responded to the tuneful harp of David, the sweet ginger of Israel.

I entered the chambers of Ecclesiastes, where the voice of the preacher was heard, and into the conservatory of Sharon: and the Lily of the Valley's sweet-scented spices filled and perfumed my life.

I entered the business office of Proverbs, and then into the observatory room of the Prophets, where I saw telescopes of various sizes pointed to far-off events, but all concentrated on the bright and morning Star.

I entered the audience room of the King of kings, and caught a vision of His glory from the standpoint of Matthew, Mark, Luke and John; and passed into the Acts of the Apostles where the Holy Spirit was doing His Work in the formation of the infant Church.

Then into the correspondence room, where sat Paul and Peter, James and John, penning their Epistles. I stepped into the throne room of Revelation, where towered glittering peaks and caught a vision of the King upon the Throne in all His glory, and I cried:

All hail the power of Jesus' Name!
Let angels prostrate fall;
Bring forth the royal diadem
And crown Him Lord of all!*

*"All Hail the Power of Jesus' Name," words by Edward Perronet, 1779; alt. by John Rippon, 1787.

———————————

——————

"With God as your heavenly Father and Him in your plans, your mind no longer magnifies the smallness of your need; you think instead of the greatness of your Father's abundance!"

——————

———————————

5

Walking by Faith

I have had some people approach me with statements like this: "I read the Bible, but I can't seem to find God's answers to my personal problems. How can I read and find my answers?"

There is a similar case in Acts 8:26-39. Here the Ethiopian eunuch was reading from the prophet Isaiah. Philip approached the chariot with a leading question:

> . . . Understandest thou what thou readest?
>
> And he said, How can I, except some man should guide me? And he desired Philip that he would come up and sit with him.
>
> The place of the scripture which he read was this, He was led as a sheep to the slaughter; and like a lamb dumb before his shearer, so opened he not his mouth: . . .
>
> Then Philip . . . began at the same scripture, and preached unto him Jesus.
>
> Acts 8:30-32,35

Although the Ethiopian eunuch was a man of great authority under Candace queen of the Ethiopians, who had the charge of all her treasure (v. 27), he was in search of truth that wealth couldn't buy. Yet, he was humble enough to allow Philip to sit up in the chariot and reveal to him what the Scriptures say about Jesus. At the right time, as he read the right Book, God sent the right man, and everything was all right!

Note here that Philip was not one of the twelve, nor did he have any claim to apostleship. He was one of the "deacons" or "elders" chosen in Acts 6:1-7 to wait on tables. But he was a preacher of the Word (Acts 8:34) and an evangelist with a godly family (Acts 21:8).

God Will Send the Guidance You Need

As in the case of the Ethiopian eunuch, you too may have difficulty in finding answers to your questions. But as you remain in God's Word and continue to be open before Him in your search, you can be assured that, at the right time, God will send someone across your path to help you. It may come through revelation, an insight that someone shares from the Word, a prophecy, a word of wisdom or other manifestation of the Spirit, but you can be sure that God will send the guidance you need, and you can be sure that He will send it at the right time.

A Word About Personal Prophecy

Personal prophecy in itself should not be your answer, but only a confirmation of what God has already impressed upon your spirit. Through the Word and through prayer, you will sense in your spirit what is right. Most especially when a word comes from a person who isn't acquainted with you and tells you what God has already shown you, then *step out and the Lord will direct you further.*

Know also that a prophecy can be true but still not intended to change your direction or alter the course of action you have received from God. We see this in the case of Agabus' prophecy to Paul:

44

> And as we tarried there many days, there came down from Judaea a certain prophet, named Agabus.
>
> And when he was come unto us, he took Paul's girdle, and bound his own hands and feet, and said, Thus saith the Holy Ghost, So shall the Jews at Jerusalem bind the man that owneth this girdle, and shall deliver him into the hands of the Gentiles.
>
> And when we heard these things, both we, and they of that place, besought him not to go up to Jerusalem.
>
> Then Paul answered, What mean ye to weep and to break mine heart? for I am ready not to be bound only, but also to die at Jerusalem for the name of the Lord Jesus.
>
> And when he would not be persuaded, we ceased, saying, The will of the Lord be done.
>
> Acts 21:10-14

The rest of the book of Acts shows that even though Agabus' prophecy was true, it was not God's will for Paul to change his direction because of it.

According to Paul's own teachings, prophecy is for **edification, and exhortation, and comfort** (1 Cor. 14:3). And **we know in part, and we prophesy in part** (1 Cor. 13:9).

God knows *all*. In this instance, He gave Agabus a portion of His knowledge and, through this "word of knowledge," exhorted Paul about the future. Those standing by didn't see the full scope of Paul's mission at that time and couldn't understand why he insisted on going to Jerusalem despite what a true prophet was saying. It was after this, however, that Paul appeared before Felix, before Festus, before Agrippa, appealed to Caesar, and went on to Rome, where he wrote six books of the New Testament! How thankful we should be that Paul considered his personal calling and direction from God to be greater than the opinions of men. What a lesson this should teach us today about being led by the Spirit.

God Wants To Answer the Questions of Believers

There are many questions confronting believers today:

"When should I take my trip?"

"Should I go by plane or car?"

"What shall I wear?"

"Where should I work?"

"Whom shall I marry?"

"Must I continue school or begin my profession now?"

"Is it right to quit my job?"

"Shall I enter full-time ministry?"

"What church shall I attend?"

An endless list of questions seems to confront Christians for which the Bible doesn't always give clear and direct answers.

What's the solution in such cases?

Jesus gave the ultimate guideline in Matthew, chapter six. He defined the Christian life as a *life of faith* (Matt. 6:30), thus eliminating many unnecessary questions:

> **Therefore take no thought, saying, What shall we eat? or, What shall we drink? or, Wherewithal shall we be clothed?**

**(For after all these things do the Gentiles seek:)
for your heavenly Father knoweth that ye have need
of all these things.**
                                                    Matthew 6:31,32

Jesus promised an attitude of trust and confidence
will be your rule of life as you get your priorities in
proper order:

**But seek ye first the kingdom of God, and his
righteousness; and all these things shall be added
unto you.**
                                                         Matthew 6:33

One must realize that God's kingdom is where
Jesus is (Luke 17:21; Rom. 14:17; John 10:30), and as
you feel your heart free from all condemnation, you
can stand before God and receive the desires of your
heart.

When you put *first* things *first* with God, many
day-by-day problems will be sorted out as a matter of
course:

**Take therefore no thought for the morrow: for the
morrow shall take thought for the things of itself . . . .**
                                                         Matthew 6:34

When Christ said, **Take therefore no thought**, He
was comparing the lifestyle of the Christian to that of
an unbeliever. In other words, *with God as your heavenly
Father and Him in your plans, your mind no longer magnifies
the smallness of your need; you think instead on the greatness
of your Father's abundance!*

Take No Thought Does Not Mean "Make No Plans!"

To "take no thought" doesn't mean that you drift aimlessly through life with no definite goals. God places no prize on slothfulness. He says:

Go to the ant . . . consider her ways, and be wise:

[She] **Provideth her meat in the summer, and gathereth her food in the harvest.**

Proverbs 6:6,8

In comparison, God says to the one who doesn't plan:

How long will thou sleep, O sluggard? when wilt thou arise out of thy sleep?

Yet a little sleep, a little slumber, a little folding of the hands to sleep:

So shall thy poverty come . . . .

Proverbs 6:9-11

If you continue to sit and wait for "something to turn up," about all you can expect to turn up is next month's rent and more bills. Most likely, your own toes will "turn up" as you starve to death! In my opinion, *too many people mistake a life of idleness for a life of faith.*

There are certain obligations and vows — such as those to your family and their needs — which God expects you to meet with *His* help. Any tendency to shirk from these responsibilities is not faith. In fact, God says people who evade their duty to family obligations *deny the faith:*

But if any provide not for his own, and specially for those of his own house, he hath denied the faith, and is worse than an infidel.

1 Timothy 5:8

The Spirit of God will never lead you into a life of idleness. In all His Word, God never equates faith with inactivity or laziness. Rather, the Bible says:

**Even so, faith, if it hath not *works*, is dead . . .
I will shew thee my faith by my *works*.**
James 2:17,18

The Spirit will lead you in job situations. But don't expect Him to do the big miracles overnight. Sometimes He does, but not necessarily in the way you expect. You will find that He expects you to master the small things first, then He will lead you on to greater things:

He that is faithful in that which is least is faithful also in much . . . .
Luke 16:10a

Before David killed the giant, he had first killed a lion and a bear.

Today, if you do a good job where God has placed you, He will entrust you with more responsibility tomorrow. And never think it is unspiritual to take secular work, provided it is a wholesome vocation. This could be God's way of enlarging your witness. After all, He says, **Let your light so shine before men . . .** (Matt. 5:16); and the best place for your light to shine most brightly is in the midst of darkness!

There are Bible examples of very powerful Christians doing secular work and advancing God's kingdom through their efforts:

1. Paul made tents. (Acts 18:3.)

2. Dorcas made clothing. (Acts 9:36-39.)

3. Peter, Andrew, James and John were fishermen. (Matt. 4:18-22.)

4. Simon of Joppa was a tanner. (Acts 9:43.)

5. And Jesus was a carpenter. (Mark 6:3.)

When Christ said, **Go ye into all the world** (Mark 16:15), He not only meant the geographical land masses of the earth, but He was also referring to the world as the social order of your influence. How can we expect Him to lead us to the "heathen" of foreign lands if we don't have enough dedication to live the life among the unevangelized at home and first win them to Jesus?

At the same time, I must point out that we should continually judge ourselves and re-evaluate our priorities in life. If you can't serve God through your vocation, you had best be out of it. Sometimes it's easy to say, "I'll make a lot of money; I'll not go myself, but I will send someone else."

How far do you think Jonah got in trying to ignore the task God called *him* to do? Not very far. The men on board the ship with Jonah asked him, "What is your vocation?" (Jonah 1:8.) He could have said, "I'm on my way to Joppa to make some money; I'm going to *send* a messenger to Ninevah!" No, it wouldn't have worked. He had to go himself. God would not have accepted any *substitute!* And eventually, after much tribulation Jonah obeyed God. He went to Ninevah, spoke the words God told him to say, and the people of Ninevah repented and were spared.

Remember To Add Action to Your Faith

There is much emphasis today on faith. We define it and discuss its qualities. It's good to note, however, that faith always expresses itself in *action*. When the writer of the book of Hebrews wrote the eleventh chapter, *one* verse was devoted to the definition of faith, and the remaining *thirty-nine* verses told how faith *acts*.

It was *by faith* that . . .

Abel *offered* (v. 4),

Noah *built* (v.7),

Abraham *went* (v.8),

Sarah *conceived* (v. 11),

Isaac *blessed* (v. 20),

Jacob *worshipped* (v. 21),

Joseph *gave commandment* (v. 22),

Moses *refused, chose, esteemed,* and *forsook* (vv. 23-27).

A host of others, too numerous to mention, have put the right corresponding *actions* to their faith. I mention these examples of *active faith* to help you understand more clearly how to be led by the Spirit. The point is: *Don't just talk faith in a good confession but begin to act upon your confession.* As you do this, you will soon find yourself moving out into a broader discovery of God's plan and purpose for your individual life.

When James linked *faith's confession* with *faith's action,* he used the analogy of a bit in a horse's mouth and the rudder of a ship at sea. (James 3:2-8.)

As long as the horse stands still, the bit fulfills no practical purpose, for bits are used primarily for *guidance* while the horse is moving. If the ship is anchored or tied to the dock, regardless of how much the rudder moves, the vessel itself doesn't respond.

This illustrates how people can hear the Word, confess it with their mouth, and then not see the desired results in their lives. The reason it doesn't work is because the confession of a person's tongue is similar to the rudder of a ship. God designed it to work only as you — just like a ship — weigh anchor, dare to face the winds of adversity, and hoist your sails upon the seas of life!

Remember this: Faith is *expecting* God to do what He said in His Word He would do. Obedience is acting on God's Word and doing what His Word says to do, no matter what your circumstances may say.

"This is what makes the Spirit-led life so rewarding and so worth the living. You not only develop confidence in God and the integrity of His Word; you come to realize that God also has confidence in you! He believes in you enough to leave certain choices up to you, knowing that He will receive the glory from your life as you do what is right."

6

You Are Special With God

In 1978, one of the most severe winters on record virtually paralyzed much of northeastern America. Snow storms continued one after another for weeks.

As the blanket of snow thickened, it provided a graphic illustration of God's *versatility* and attention to *individual* detail. In all the massive snow drifts that accumulated across the nation, not one snowflake was like another! It's a divine plan, and a scientific fact, that *each individual snowflake has its own shape and design.* There were literally billions upon multiplied billions of snowflakes in this storm!

Is it any wonder then, that the same God who designs the snowflakes one by one has a unique plan and purpose for *your* individual life?

Yes, as sure as your fingerprints have a pattern of their own and can be used to identify only *you*, that's how special God sees *you* in His overall plan for the world.

For this reason, you shouldn't think it strange when situations confront you which seem to have no ready answers. God planned it that way — all for His glory. He knows that He can trust you, for you are . . .

> . . . **his workmanship, created in Christ Jesus unto good works . . . .**
>
> **Ephesians 2:10**

Therefore, be sensitive to God's voice, knowing that He deals with you on an individual basis. He may not always speak in the way you expect, but He will use different methods to guide you.

In First Kings 19:11-18, we see an example of Elijah hearing from God and being led by Him from a state of despair to a position of new hope and victory. In this case, God didn't use the obvious manifestation of the wind, the earthquake or the fire. He chose to speak in a still, small voice.

In most cases, you will find that God uses an inner witness — a peace or rest that comes to your spirit, causing you to know His presence is leading you into certain courses of action. Yet, He may choose to speak in an audible voice from time to time.

Sometimes, You Will Hear God Speak

When I first came to Tulsa, Oklahoma, to be a professor at Oral Roberts University, the devil attacked me with a sense of condemnation. I remember getting out of the car and feeling so unworthy in all the surroundings of that beautiful campus. The devil said: "You're just a foreigner; you don't have enough training; you don't have the background for this sort of thing!"

I stood there looking — feeling that I could go no further. I looked up at the sky where clouds were boiling up over the O.R.U. Prayer Tower. A message came to me so strong. It was as an audible voice saying: "Son, what are you doing? I have brought you to this place. I love you as much as I love Oral Roberts, and in My eyes you are just as beautiful. I called you to do a different work, but I am not a respecter of persons.''

I felt such a surge of power at that moment that I literally ran across that field, and from that day forward, I have been free of all condemnation and feelings of unworthiness.

Later, after I had launched out in personal ministry, I was in a series of meetings in Blackwell, Oklahoma, when the devil tried to attack me with a severe sickness. I was praying, believing, and asking: "Why, Lord, is this coming upon me?"

While praying and reading God's Word, I fell asleep. One of my associates and his wife were in the room next to mine, and I thought I heard him come into the room. A voice said: "You are already healed!"

I woke up. There was no one there. As I closed my eyes again, the voice thundered: *"I have already healed you!"*

I realized that God had spoken. I hit the floor with both feet, shouting. All sickness and pain were gone. I was completely healed!

So God may choose to speak in an audible voice, but, as a rule, His Spirit bears witness with your inner spirit. When He does speak, the main thing is: *let Him speak!* Be determined to *know your Father's voice* through the process of learning His written Word.

Hear God Speak Through His Word

Look again at those (in Heb. 11) who *acted* on their faith. Notice, that in many instances, there had been no precedent. In Noah's case, no one had ever built an ark before, so there was no established pattern for him to follow.

About Abraham, the Bible says:

> **By faith . . . he went out,** *not knowing* **whither he went.**
>
> **Hebrews 11:8**

You must also realize that in most instances there is **a due season** for God's plan. (Gal. 6:9.) Until that time comes, you must continue to act in blind obedience to the principles of God's Word. Abraham simply took the first step, believing God to direct each succeeding step. He had no precedent to guide him, and there was no one but God to show him the way.

Although Abraham acted in obedience **not knowing whither he went** (Heb. 11:8), there were certain principles that governed his actions, always guiding him in harmony with God's Word. The Spirit will never lead you contrary to the Scriptures. *Remember this:* the will of God will never lead you into a situation where the grace and power of God cannot keep you.

In Africa, I was confronted with what — in the natural — appeared to be impossible situations. I was preaching to a huge congregation when suddenly a belligerent fellow stood up. He antagonistically asked, ''Will the God of the white man heal my black brother?''

It was a case where words were not enough. I've found that you can talk all you want to some people, but what they need is a real demonstration of God's love. All at once, the Spirit of God prompted me to step into the large audience. I was impressed to lay my hands on a woman who had a large growth on her belly. As I prayed for this black lady, the people saw the growth vanish before their eyes. They realized that Jesus loves blacks and whites alike. They believed and responded to my appeal to get right with God. The man who had startled everyone with his unusual question was convinced of the truth of God's Word.

There was also a man from Uganda, possessed with demons. He was yelling and had the strength of three large men. His hands and feet were tied, and he had a bench on top of him. Yet, he was throwing the bench and the three men about as though the men were children and the bench a toy.

I've learned through experience that when you don't know what to do, begin to act on Romans 8:26,28 and pray in the Spirit, and **the Spirit itself maketh intercession . . . according to the will of God** in you with the perfect solution to every dilemma. As I prayed in my heavenly language, a powerful anointing came upon me. Stepping forward boldly, I laid my hands on the man and commanded the demons to go in Jesus' name. To my surprise, nothing happened.

Then God said: "Go back and continue preaching. You did your part; now I will do My part!"

Today that man is saved, completely sane and teaching school in Africa. I did all I could, then God finished the job, just as His Word declares. Like Abraham, I acted in faith, in all the light God had given me, and He did the rest.

On another occasion, I received a phone call from a desperate father asking me to come to his home in a different city and pray for his thirty-five year old son who was possessed and controlled by evil spirits. The man was so violent that neither his father nor his family could physically subdue him or control him, and they were all afraid of him. As I was speaking to the father on the phone, the Lord began to impress on my spirit that I should not go there and be on his territory, but that he should come to church and be on my territory. The father of the boy was not pleased with my decision and said to me, "What kind of a Christian are you! Why won't you come and help my son?" My reply to him was, "Whatever the Lord instructs me, that is what I do, and the Lord impressed me to tell you that if you want your son to be free, then you have to come with him to church."

That week we were having our mid-week service, and I had one of our ushers run in to me saying, "There is a crazy man in the back of a car!" He was naked, and they had his hands and feet tied with wires. I went outside, and I saw in the back of the car a naked man with three adult men holding him down in the back seat. The father asked me to pray for him and deliver him in the back seat of the car. The Lord impressed me again to have him come and be in the service. When I advised the father of this, he replied, "But he is naked!" One of the deacons brought a blanket, and we wrapped the blanket about him and brought him into the church to sit in the back row.

I proceeded with the service, and the man began to growl like a wild animal. I instructed the congregation not to be frightened or to pay attention, but to listen to the Word. Approximately fifteen minutes into the service, the Lord instructed me to go and pray for him and cast the spirit out. As I approached the man, he began to growl and foam at the mouth. As I attempted to put my hand on his head, he snapped at me like a mad dog. At that moment, I said, "Lord, how do you want me to handle this?" The lord instructed me to bind the spirit of rage, put my hand on his head and cast the spirit of lunacy out of him. As I did that, the man fell backwards like a wilted flower, and he opened his eyes and began to cry and thank me for delivering him from his condition. The man was marvelously saved, filled with the Holy Spirit and glorified God for delivering him.

Learn From Abraham's Walk of Faith

As you look at Abraham's example of faith, you can see an established guideline in which you will never go astray:

1. *He obeyed.* (Heb. 11:8.) Like Abraham, you, too, must move in obedience to God's command. The New Testament leaves no doubt about His will for you as a Christian. You must accept Christ as your Lord with all your heart and seek to put Him first in all your life. You must love your neighbor as yourself. You must obey Christ's commission to evangelize the world — whether your witness be across the seas or across the street. This was the rule of life for the early-day believers and apostles. Although there were times when they didn't fully understand with their minds about every situation, they continued strong in their allegiance to Christ and their devotion to His cause.

2. *He went out.* (Heb. 11:8.) Abraham's progress was always in the direction in which God called him, away from the old lifestyle and the old country from which he separated himself. He refused to think on

the old life, but began to think *new* thoughts, renewing his mind daily in his walk with God. Thus, there was no opportunity for him to go back:

> **And truly, if they have been mindful of that country from whence they came out, they might have had opportunity to have returned.**
>
> **Hebrews 11:15**

3. *He looked for God's promise to be fulfilled.* (Heb. 11:10.) In your walk with God, you must *expect* Him to keep His Word. Continually *look* for His answers. Praise Him for His promises, believing Him to make them good in *your* life. In this attitude of faith and trust, you have His favor:

> **For he that cometh to God must believe that he [God] is, and that he is a *rewarder* of them that diligently seek him.**
>
> **Hebrews 11:6b**

In other words, let your faith be rooted in more than the fact of God's existence, *that He is.* Believe, instead, that He *is* what He *is* — a *Rewarder!*

To God, You Are Special

God sees you as a *special* person and will deal with you on an *individual* basis. He doesn't just wind you up like a toy soldier or mechanical robot. He doesn't feed truth into you from tapes and program you for service as though you were a modern-day computer. Nor does He want you to respond like a trained animal, imitating only what others have done.

You are different from all of the above. In fact, there is no one else exactly like you. You are unique. You have an *individual will* and have been divinely given the power of *personal choice.* Because of this, *you* alone determine the glory that God receives from your life and the pleasure you will receive from serving Him.

This is what makes the Spirit-led life so worth the living. You not only develop confidence in God and the integrity of His Word; you come to realize that *God also has confidence in you!* He believes in you enough to leave certain choices up to you, knowing that He will receive glory from your life as you do what is right. When in doubt, you learn to voluntarily seek out His plan by always continuing steadfast in the Word of Truth.

> I will worship toward thy holy temple, and praise thy name for thy lovingkindness and for thy truth: for thou hast magnified thy word above all thy name.
>
> **Psalms 138:2**

> Then said the Lord unto me, . . . I will hasten my word to perform it.
>
> **Jeremiah 1:12**

―――――――――

――――

*"We must come to know (through the Bible)
our responsibilities and positions
in interpersonal relationships:
husbands to wives, wives to husbands;
parents to children, children to
parents; and employer to employee,
employee to employer."*

――――

―――――――――

7

Love: Your Practical Guide

As you prepare for God's guidance, a basic fact to remember is: *the Spirit will never lead you out of one situation unless God has something better prepared for you.*

Often, I've had well-meaning and sincere Christians tell me they were leaving their jobs or changing their positions in life with no definite leading toward anything else. Then some people question if they should join or attend a particular church, if they should enter the full-time ministry, etc.

In some cases, the fight of faith is more intense than in others. The solution doesn't immediately come as we search God's Word. However, even though the final solution isn't clear, the Word will give you direction and strengthen your faith, establishing definite principles from which your choice is to be made. Therefore, have a firm determination that . . .

> **This book** [the Bible] **. . . shall not depart out of thy mouth; but thou shalt meditate therein day and night, that thou mayest observe to do according to all that is written therein: for then thou shalt make thy way prosperous, and then thou shalt have good success.**
>
> **Joshua 1:8**

It is true that the Holy Spirit will guide you into all truth, but you alone must choose or decide your destiny. By the choices you make, you are the one who determines whether or not your *way is prosperous* or if you have *good success*. Life itself cannot give you love, peace, and joy unless you really will it. Life will give you time and place; it's up to you to fill it. God does give the inner promptings and the inclinations of the heart. As you are sincere and open before Him, you can sense His approval in your spirit as He "guides you with His eye . . ."

> **I will instruct thee and teach thee in the way which thou shalt go: I will guide thee with mine eye.**
> **Psalm 32:8**

Your prayers, your actions and your direction should always be definite and decisive:

> **But let him ask in faith, nothing wavering. For he that wavereth is like a wave of the sea driven with the wind and tossed.**

> **For let not that man think that he shall receive any thing of the Lord.**

> **A double minded man is unstable in all his ways.**
> **James 1:6-8**

God Desires Balance

Many Christians make a tragic mistake, especially young believers, when they rely totally on the inward voice of the Spirit within them to decide and direct everything they do. The inner prompting of the Spirit does seem to offer a closer intimacy with God, but in reality and practice, this desire for "super-spirituality" leads only to frustration, bewilderment and tragedy. True guidance comes when we honor the Holy Spirit as our Guide *and* when we honor the Holy Scriptures through which the Holy Spirit guides us.

> **Howbeit when he, the Spirit of truth, is come,
> he will guide you into all truth: for he shall not speak
> of himself; but whatsoever he shall hear, that shall
> he speak . . . .**
>
> **John 16:13**

Understand also that the Holy Spirit not only uses the Scriptures to reveal truth in a clear and definite revelation through the Bible, but He also helps you to understand the nature and character of God. The Scriptures instill basic convictions, attitudes, ideals and value-judgments that establish guidelines for your everyday life. This isn't altogether a matter of inward prompting apart from the Word, but a revelation of God's character and will which the Holy Spirit reveals to us through the Word and helps us understand how to apply these principles to our lives.

The basic form of divine guidance, therefore, is the Holy Spirit's scriptural presentation to us of positive ideas which exhort, edify and comfort us, giving to us vital guidelines for all our living. We must learn to be the kind of person that Jesus was. We must seek His virtues and practice them to the limit. We must come to know, through the Word, our responsibilities and positions in inter-human relationships: husbands to wives, wives to husbands; parents to children, children to parents; and employee to employer, employer to employee.

One practical way that the Holy Spirit guides us through the Word is by helping us to understand our right relationship to God and to each other:

> **And whatsoever ye do in word or deed, do all in
> the name of the Lord Jesus, giving thanks to God and
> the Father by him.**

Wives, submit yourselves unto your own husbands, as it is fit in the Lord.

Husbands, love your wives, and be not bitter against them.

Children, obey your parents in all things: for this is well pleasing unto the Lord.

Fathers, provoke not your children to anger, lest they be discouraged.

Servants, obey in all things your masters according to the flesh; not with eyeservice, as menpleasers; but in singleness of heart, fearing God:

And whatsoever ye do, do it heartily, as to the Lord, and not unto men;

Knowing that of the Lord ye shall receive the reward of the inheritance: for ye serve the Lord Christ.
Colossians 3:17-24

All That Glitters Isn't Gold

A few years ago, I went through a trying time where I learned a great lesson on spiritual priorities. I discovered: "All that glitters isn't gold."

It was when I first came to Oral Roberts University. We were having a financial struggle, and I was really seeking God about our needs. During this time a man from an oil company contacted the university. He wanted to know if there was anyone there who could translate English into Russian. The company had large contracts with the Soviet Union and needed a capable translator. He was referred to me.

"Mr. Basansky," the oil executive said, "we will pay you twenty-five cents a word to translate our manuscripts into Russian."

Right away, I began to add it all up. My mind was clicking away like a computer: "And . . . but . . . to . . . it . . . nor . . . for — at twenty-five cents a word, that's already a dollar and fifty cents!"

I plunged myself into that project with all my available time. I must confess now that it was not so much out of *need* that I did it, but more because of *greed*. After a week, I was exhausted and couldn't understand why. I began to seek God in earnest: "Lord," I said, "I know this is of You . . . "

"Are you sure?"

It was a searching question from heaven that cut straight into my heart.

"Yes, Lord — You promised to bless me financially and to prosper me."

"No, this thing is not of Me," He gently replied. "Examine your record. How much time do you have with your family, your wife and children? How much time do you have for *Me*? How much of My Word have you read this week?"

Shamefully, I had to answer "none" to all these questions.

God asked, "How can you say I am doing this for you? Would I deprive you of all that I have already blessed you with?"

I lost no time in calling the oil company representative. "Come and get your material," I told him.

He said, "Look — money is no object! We need those translations. Just name your price!"

"I can't do it at any price," I informed him.

"Mr. Basansky, we will make you a rich man."

"No, I can't do this work. God tells me it is not His will. I don't need the money badly enough to go against His will."

Then the devil began to really show himself. The man on the other end of the line began using offensive language. But I insisted that I was through, and they came and picked up the material.

It was then that God began to open new doors for me to speak. My whole perspective had changed. No longer did I operate out of greed for gain, just to be able to say that God prospered *me*. I now saw money as a "tool" for His use, to buy tickets for speaking engagements, to supply Christian literature, to duplicate cassette tapes, to conduct overseas crusades — to advance the message of Jesus to the ends of the earth!

God's Way Is To Promote

God taught me through this experience that *He never asks you to give up one thing without offering something better in its place.*

Another important lesson I learned through this experience was that when God leads you into another field, He will also confirm it with your wife or husband. It may take a while, but as you remain faithful to His calling, He will set events into motion that will make all things work out in harmony.

The primary thrust and concern of all the Bible is that we serve God and put Him first in all things:

> **Let us hear the conclusion of the whole matter: Fear God, and keep his commandments: for this is the whole duty to man.**
>
> **Ecclesiastes 12:13**

Jesus said:

> **. . . Thou shalt love the Lord thy God with all thy heart, and with all thy soul, and with all thy mind.**
>
> **This is the first and great commandment.**
>
> **And the second is like unto it, Thou shalt love thy neighbour as thyself.**
>
> **Matthew 22:37-39**

As you study the ten commandments, you see that they are divided into two categories: *our relationship to God* and *our relationship to our fellowman*.

Jesus Taught the Love Commandments

Jesus said that the two *Love Commandments* that He gave are the sum total of all:

> **On these two commandments hang all the law and the prophets.**
>
> **Matthew 22:40**

Then Paul said:

> **. . . he that loveth another hath fulfilled the law.**
>
> **Romans 13:8**

> **For all the law is fulfilled in one word, even in this; Thou shalt love thy neighbour as thyself.**
>
> **Galatians 5:14**

The Spirit-filled life is an absolute requirement in our walk with God because it is only through *love* that we can fulfill our duty to God and our responsibilities

71

to others. This is possible only as we allow the Spirit to control our lives:

> . . . because the *love* of God is shed abroad in our hearts by the Holy Ghost . . . .
>
> **Romans 5:5**

———————

———

"A good rule of life is: live as though Christ were returning today, but plan as though He will not return in your lifetime. In other words, plan your life — in God's will; then live your plan — as God wills."

———

———————

8

Obstacles to the Spirit-Led Life and How To Overcome Them

To be led by the Spirit into the fullness of God's plan and purpose for your life, it is necessary that you recognize some of the obstacles that Satan puts in the Christian's path.

First: To be led by the Spirit of God, you must make sure your speech and thought patterns are in harmony with the Word of God. (Matt. 12:37; Prov. 6:2; 18:20,21.)

> **Let no corrupt communication proceed out of your mouth, but that which is good to the use of edifying, that it may minister grace unto the hearers.**
>
> **And grieve not the holy Spirit of God . . .**
>
> **Let all bitterness, and wrath, and anger, and clamour, and evil speaking, be put away from you, with all malice:**
>
> **And be ye kind one to another, tenderhearted, forgiving one another, even as God for Christ's sake hath forgiven you.**
>
> **Ephesians 4:29-32**

Second: Know that you are made in the image and likeness of God, and as David said, you are **fearfully and wonderfully made** (Ps. 139:14).

> **And God said, Let us make man in our image, after our likeness: and let them have dominion over**

> the fish of the sea, and over the fowl of the air, and over the cattle, and over all the earth, and over every creeping thing that creepeth upon the earth.
>
> So God created man in his own image, in the image of God created he him; male and female created he them.
>
> **Genesis 1:26,27**

Being in the image of God, there are certain responsibilities that you must face that require diligent thought and personal planning on your part. In these, God will help you, but He expects you to take the initiative. For example, God made the earth, but He gave man the ability to **subdue it: and have dominion** over it (Gen. 1:28); God made the animals, but it was man's responsibility to name them, and he did so from the high power of intellect that God placed within him:

> And out of the ground the Lord God formed every beast of the field, and every fowl of the air; and brought them unto Adam to see what he would call them: and whatsoever Adam called every living creature, that was the name thereof.
>
> **Genesis 2:19**

We might note here that Adam simply assumed his God-given responsibility and *did* what he was created to *do*. God's plan for his life was *already* revealed, and God observed man to see what he would call them. And whatsoever Adam called the animals, God said: *"That's good enough for Me; that's what it will be!"*

It's been said: *For man to try to do what only God Himself can do is a waste of effort; for man to ask God to do what God has already told him to do is a waste of prayer.*

Many people aren't willing, or haven't the courage, to apply themselves in the realm of Spirit-led, intelligent thinking. Instead, they continue to pray about what God has already commissioned them to do, depending entirely upon an inner feeling to guide them and at times even to supply momentum. This is a grave mistake that can lead you into all sorts of error. You must realize that, in Christ, you have been restored to the place Adam occupied before the fall. In Christ, you *have dominion* over God's creation, and in His presence, you can make intelligent decisions that bring honor to Him.

> **Now therefore thus saith the Lord of hosts; Consider your ways.**
>
> **Haggai 1:5**

He says:

> **O that they that were wise, that they understood this, that they would consider . . . .**
>
> **Deuteronomy 32:29**

Third: Another area of danger that many Christians face is the unwillingness to plan ahead. Planning ahead is a vital part of successful, Spirit-led living. It was sanctioned by Jesus Himself in Luke 14:28:

> **For which of you, intending to build a tower, sitteth not down first, and counteth the cost, whether he have sufficient to finish it?**

A good rule of life is: *live* as though Christ were returning today but *plan* as though he will not return in your lifetime. In other words, *plan your life* — in God's will; and then *live your plan* — as God wills.

> **For that ye *ought* to say, If the Lord will, *we shall live*, and *do* this, or that.**
>
> **James 4:15**

What is the "this or that" which *you* have purposed to *do* — in God's will? Set your goals, make

make your plans, and God will help you see them through. (Prov. 29:18.)

Fourth: A critical area of fallacy for many Christians is their unwillingness to take advice. The Scripture is emphatic on this need. The Bible says:

> **The way of a fool is right in his own eyes: but he that hearkeneth unto counsel is wise.**
> **Proverbs 12:15**

A person who is not willing to listen to advice is immature, proud, and very stubborn. To make major decisions, it is vital that you rely on good advice:

> **Where no counsel is, the people fall: but in the multitude of counsellors there is safety.**
> **Proverbs 11:14**

It would be good, especially for those young in the faith to take the advice of Peter:

> **Likewise, ye younger, submit yourselves unto the elder. Yea, all of you be subject one to another, and be clothed with humility: for God resisteth the proud, and giveth grace to the humble.**
> **1 Peter 5:5**

In another chapter, I spoke of the ministry gifts which God has placed in the church and the importance they have in your Spirit-led life. Yet, it is also scriptural for you to observe the lives of those godly men and women who have walked in the way before you, who are veterans in spiritual warfare. Listen to them, and you will learn many lessons of faith that will keep you from future dangers and snares of the enemy. I realize there are always people who know more about certain subjects or things than you or I, and even if we cannot fully accept all they say, nothing but good can come from carefully weighing their advice and counsel.

Fifth: One of the most difficult obstacles for people to hurdle is their unwillingness to examine or judge themselves.

Often we dislike being realistic with ourselves, and we do not know ourselves as well as we should. We can recognize certain pitfalls in others but fail to see them in ourselves. We need to ask ourselves why we feel that we are so right and *why* we should take a particular course of action. We must be honest with ourselves and give ourselves reasons for each decision we make. Be willing to ask yourself these questions:

1. Would Jesus do what I am about to do?

2. Would Jesus say what I am about to say?

3. Would Jesus act the way I am about to act?

If the answer is no, then you, too, must not.

It is always wise to lay the case before someone whom we respect as an upright Christian and whose judgment we trust. We also need to keep praying even as the psalmist prayed:

Search me, O God, and know my heart: try me, and know my thoughts:

And see if there be any wicked way in me, and lead me in the way everlasting.

Psalm 139:23,24

Sixth: Beware of a deep personal drawing or attachment to any individual and be willing to face the fact that they are still human; don't idolize them or their teachings, and don't let them or their teachings have priority over Christ and the Word.

Those Christians who have not been made aware of the pride and self-deception in their own lives cannot detect these things in others. And this has made it possible, from time to time, for well-meaning Christians to fall under the spell of those who are proud and who seek to gain popularity and self-esteem, having no consideration for others. They think only of themselves, and are able to manipulate the Word of God for their own benefit. Thus, many Christians easily fall under their influence and don't back-track them, inspect their fruits (Gal. 5:22) and try their spirits as commanded by the Word of God:

> Beloved, believe not every spirit, but try the spirits whether they are of God: because many false prophets are gone out into the world.
>
> Hereby know ye the Spirit of God: Every spirit that confesseth that Jesus Christ is come in the flesh is of God:
>
> And every spirit that confesseth not that Jesus Christ is come in the flesh is not of God.
>
> 1 John 4:1-3a
>
> Beware of false prophets, which come to you in sheep's clothing, but inwardly they are ravening wolves.
>
> Ye shall know them by their fruits. Do men gather grapes of thorns, or figs of thistles?
>
> Even so every good tree bringeth forth good fruit; but a corrupt tree bringeth forth evil fruit.
>
> A good tree cannot bring forth evil fruit, neither can a corrupt tree bring forth good fruit. Wherefore by their fruits ye shall know them.
>
> Matthew 7:15-18,20
>
> I [Jesus] am the good shepherd: the good shepherd giveth his life for the sheep.

> **But he that is an hireling, and not the shepherd, whose own the sheep are not, seeth the wolf coming, and leaveth the sheep, and fleeth: and the wolf catcheth them, and scattereth the sheep.**
>
> **John 10:11,12**

Even when many gifted, dynamic, magnetic men are aware of the danger of "personality cults" and try to avoid this danger, they are not always able to stop Christian people from treating them as angels or elevating them in their minds as "super-prophets." These sincere, but misguided, Christians take the words of these individuals as guidance and blindly follow their leading. But God would have you to know that this is not the way to be led by the Holy Spirit. Outstanding men are not necessarily wrong; but they are not necessarily right either. They and their views must be respected, yet they, nor their teachings, are to be idolized or considered infallible. Nor are their statements to be substituted for the Word of God. The Bible admonishes us to . . .

> **Prove all things; hold fast that which is good.**
>
> **1 Thessalonians 5:21**

> **Proving what is acceptable unto the Lord.**
>
> **Ephesians 5:10**

Seventh: Another problem area for Christians is their failure to see that God has a due season for them to reap His blessings and to experience His guidance in detail:

> **And let us not be weary in well doing: for in due season we shall reap, if we faint not.**
>
> **Galatians 6:9**

81

Wherefore gird up the loins of your mind, be sober, and hope to the end for the grace that is to be brought unto you at the revelation of Jesus Christ.

1 Peter 1:13

In other words, don't get in a hurry. *Wait on the Lord* is a constant refrain throughout the Word of God:

But they that wait upon the Lord shall renew their strength; they shall mount up with wings as eagles; they shall run, and not be weary; and they shall walk, and not faint.

Isaiah 40:31

(See also Ps. 52:9; 37:7; 40:1.)

The Christian's path of progress is a constant upwardly spiraling cycle of *waiting* on the Lord, *mounting up on wings* as eagles (in full strength), *running* and not being weary (as the strength lessens), and *walking* without fainting — *then* it's time to *wait on the Lord* all over again, as the cycle repeats itself. There are times when your spiritual experiences are higher than other times, but remember this: *even at your lowest, your valleys are higher than the sinner's mountain tops!*

That is why Paul admonishes believers to:

. . . remember . . . that at that time ye were without Christ . . . strangers from the covenants of promise, having no hope, and without God in the world.

Ephesians 2:11,12

God is never in a hurry as we are, and it is not His way to give more light on the future than we need for our action in the present, or to guide us more than one step at a time. I've often used the illustration of driving my car from Tulsa to Oklahoma City at night. My lights don't show a clear road as in the daytime; I can see only several yards at a time. Yet, as I drive farther and need it, the light is always there ahead of me to show me the way.

A good rule for every Christian should be: when in doubt, when confused, when not sure, do nothing at all but continue to read God's Word and wait on the Lord. When God is ready and action is needed, light will come, and you will know that it is God.

Eighth: It is important that you realize that your difficulties and problems don't necessarily mean you are going in the wrong direction. Paul linked *persecution* and *affliction* with *faith* and *doctrine,* saying:

> But thou hast fully known my doctrine, manner of life, purpose, faith, longsuffering, charity, patience, persecutions, afflictions . . . what persecutions I endured: but out of them all the Lord delivered me.
>
> 2 Timothy 3:10,11

Then he said:

> Yea, and *all* that will live godly in Christ Jesus shall suffer persecution.
>
> 2 Timothy 3:12

> Beloved, think it not strange concerning the fiery trial which is to try you, as though some strange thing happened unto you:
>
> But *rejoice,* inasmuch as ye are partakers of Christ's sufferings . . .
>
> If ye be reproached for the name of Christ, *happy* are ye; for the spirit of glory and of God resteth upon you . . . .
>
> 1 Peter 4:12-14

Many Christians grow anxious because of the problems that arise. They have started on their journey because they sincerely believed that divine guidance was given then run into a brand new set of troubles.

They run into isolation, criticism, abandonment by their family or friends and just plain frustration of all sorts.

At such times, some people immediately think of the trouble that Jonah had when he ran from God (Jonah 1:3), and think that perhaps something is wrong in their lives. They remember how Jonah was supposed to go east and preach at Ninevah, but instead took a ship going north to Tarsus. He was caught in the storm, thrown overboard and swallowed by a great fish. Through this well-known series of events, God allowed Jonah to be brought to his senses.

Remember this: Trouble never comes from God our Father but from the trouble-maker, the devil, when we allow him to put it on us. Christians should never praise God for their troubles. However, they must not forget to praise God — even when they are *in* trouble — and God will deliver them. (Acts 16:23-26.)

Certainly, when a Christian runs into trouble, he should stop and examine his motives, consider his ways and see if there is anything in his personal life that displeases God. Yet, at the same time, trouble doesn't always mean you are off track. The Bible says:

> **Many are the afflictions of the righteous: but the Lord delivereth him out of them all.**
>
> **The Lord redeemeth the soul of his servants: and none of them that trust in him shall be desolate.**
>
> **Psalm 34:19,22**

Don't Be Fleeced by a Fleece

I would interject here that no Christian should be led by a sign or what is sometimes called a fleece. Many people look at the story of Gideon, where he tested

God's guidance by placing a piece of wool — a fleece — on the ground. (Judg. 6.) First, he asked God to cause the fleece to be wet and the ground around it to be dry; next, he asked for the fleece to remain dry, while the ground around it was made wet with dew. Taking a single Scripture out of context and developing it into its own doctrine can lead to trouble! The idea of putting out a fleece has been given a workout by some who seek to know for certain they are in God's will. Sometimes Christians act completely contrary to the principle represented in the story of Gideon, saying they are fleecing God.

Notice that Gideon already had God's Word — so the fleece was meaningless as far as direction was concerned. The fact that the ground was wet or dry — neither helped or hindered Gideon from doing what God said do. That's entirely different than the so-called fleeces people put out today. One might say, "Lord — if it's Your will for me to go to Africa, send me $1,000." What if it wasn't God's will for you to go to Africa, yet you still needed $1,000 for something else? Your foolish fleece would tie God's hands and rob you of that financial blessing. Another person might say, "Lord, if it's Your will for me to enter full-time ministry, save two souls through my witness today." Well, the Bible says it's *always* God's will to save the lost, whether or not you ever enter full-time ministry.

Do you see what I'm talking about? A fleece will lead you into trouble, but the Spirit of God will always lead you into victory!

As God's children, we should never put our trust in a fleece. The Bible says:

For as many as are led by the Spirit of God, they are the sons of God.

Romans 8:14

Jesus set the example for us, by trusting the Holy Spirit even to His death on the cross. We should never try any substitute for this Power that He has promised us.

Sometimes Christians who are doing the work of God may see an obstacle or detour in their path and get all shook up, not knowing what to do. Even in the natural, when you are driving down the road and see a detour, you don't just stop in the middle of the road, throw your hands up and say you can go no further. The detour in the road doesn't mean that it is the end of your journey. You must follow the directions the detour gives you, and you will always come back to the right path. (Ps. 119:105,130.)

It is the same when a Christian wakes up to the fact that he has missed God's guidance and taken the wrong way. Is the damage unforgivable? Must you be put off course for life? *Praise God, no!* You don't have to! Our God does not merely forgive us. He also restores our relationship with Him. This is part of the wonder of God's grace and sovereignty. He promises:

And I will restore to you the years that the locust hath eaten, the cankerworm, and the caterpillar, and the palmerworm . . . .

And ye shall eat in plenty, and be satisfied, and praise the name of the Lord your God, that hath dealt wondrously with you.

Joel 2:25,26a

Jesus, Who restored Peter after his denial and continued to correct his course (Acts 10; Gal. 2), is our

Lord today. He is the same. He has not changed. Through Him and His victory, God makes not only the wrath of men to turn to His praise, but the misadventures of Christians also!

> But where sin abounded, grace did much more abound.
>
> **Romans 5:20b**

> And if any man sin, we have an advocate with the Father, Jesus Christ the righteous.
>
> And he is the propitiation for our sins; and not for ours only, but also for the sins of the whole world.
>
> **1 John 2:1b,2**

When you make a mistake, repent! Don't run away *from the Light!* Run back *to* the Light!

> But if we walk in the light, as he is in the light, we have fellowship one with another, and the blood of Jesus Christ his Son cleanseth us from all sin.
>
> If we confess our sins, he is faithful and just to forgive us our sins, and to cleanse us from all unrighteousness.
>
> **1 John 1:7,9**

"The Bible tells how the Holy Spirit manifested Himself in many other ways. Yet, the following twenty examples are given as a cross-section to encourage you not to limit His wonder-working power to any pre-conceived ideas. Realize that His power is promised to every believer."

9

How the Holy Spirit Works
To Fulfill God's Plan

From the first chapter in Genesis, when **the spirit of God moved upon the face of the waters** (Gen. 1:2), until God's last altar call in Revelation, where **the Spirit and the bride say, Come . . . take the water of life freely** (Rev. 22:17), we read how the Holy Spirit works to carry out God's plans and purposes. A review of some biblical accounts will acquaint you with the nature and work of the Holy Spirit and help you to cooperate with His mission in the world, enabling you to be led by Him into all Truth.

First: At creation, the Holy Spirit brought order out of chaos, revealing from the very beginning that His mission is one of harmony and unity.

> **And the earth was without form, and void; and darkness was upon the face of the deep. And the spirit of God moved upon the face of the waters.**
> **Genesis 1:2**

Second: Through the Spirit, God created man in His own image:

> **And the Lord God formed man of the dust of the ground, and breathed into his nostrils the breath of life; and man became a living soul.**
> **Genesis 2:7**

Thou sendest forth thy spirit, they are created....
Psalm 104:30

The spirit of God hath made me, and the breath
of the Almighty hath given me life.

Job 33:4

Third: Through the help of the Holy Spirit, Moses and the elders of Israel gave upright judgment and possessed physical strength far beyond natural ability. Numbers 11:10-25 says:

> **And the Lord came down in a cloud, and spake unto him [Moses], and took of the spirit that was upon him, and gave it unto the seventy elders: and it came to pass, that, when the spirit rested upon them, they prophesied, and did not cease.**

Fourth: The Holy Spirit filled the workers of the tabernacle with wisdom and knowledge, enabling them to make material things beyond the conception of ordinary man:

> **... I have filled him with the spirit of God, in wisdom, and in understanding, and in knowledge, and in all manner of workmanship,**
>
> **To devise cunning works, to work in gold, and in silver, and in brass,**
>
> **And in cutting of stones, to set them, and in carving of timber, to work in all manner of workmanship.**

Exodus 31:3-5

(See also Ex. 28:3 and 35:31.)

Fifth: The Holy Spirit anointed Joshua with wisdom to lead, to carry on the mission God had given to Moses:

> And Joshua the son of Nun was full of the spirit of wisdom; for Moses had laid his hands upon him: and the children of Israel hearkened unto him, and did as the Lord commanded Moses.
>
> **Deuteronomy 34:9**

Sixth: The Spirit of God was in Joseph, giving him power to interpret dreams and ability to rule:

> And Pharaoh said unto his servants, Can we find such a one as this is, a man in whom the spirit of God is?
>
> **Genesis 41:38**

(Gen. 41.)

Seventh: The Holy Spirit empowered men to prophesy:

> And there ran a young man, and told Moses, and said, Eldad and Medad do prophesy in the camp.
>
> And Moses said unto him, Enviest thou for my sake? would God that all the Lord's people were prophets, and that the Lord would put his spirit upon them!
>
> **Numbers 11:27,29**

(See also Num. 24:2; 1 Sam. 10:6-11; 19:20-23; 2 Sam. 23:2; 2 Chron. 15:1-7; 20:14-19; 24:20-23; 1 Cor. 14:5,24; Acts 2:17.)

Eighth: The Holy Spirit gives men power to impart spiritual gifts to others:

> For I long to see you, that I may impart unto you some spiritual gift . . . .
>
> **Romans 1:11**

> Neglect not the gift that is in thee, which was given thee by prophecy, with the laying on of the hands of the presbytery.
>
> **1 Timothy 4:14**

(See also 2 Tim. 1:6; Heb. 6:1,2.)

Ninth: Men were anointed for victory in battle:

> **And the spirit of the Lord came upon him . . . and his hand prevailed against Chushanrishathaim.**
>
> **Judges 3:10**

(See also Judg. 6:34; 11:29; 1 Sam. 11:6.)

Tenth: The Holy Spirit inspired people to write songs:

> **Now these be the last words of David . . . the sweet psalmist of Israel, said,**
>
> **The spirit of the Lord spake by me, and his word was in my tongue.**
>
> **2 Samuel 23:1,2**

Eleventh: Through the Holy Spirit, men received supernatural strength and a change of character:

> **Then went Samson down, and his father and his mother, to Timnath, and came to the vineyards of Timnath: and, behold, a young lion roared against him.**
>
> **And the spirit of the Lord came mightily upon him, and he rent him as he would have rent a kid, and he had nothing in his hand . . . .**
>
> **Judges 14:5,6**

(See also Judg. 13:25; 14:19; 15:14.)

Twelfth: The Holy Spirit leads believers through tests:

> **And Jesus being full of the Holy Ghost returned from Jordan, and was led by the Spirit into the wilderness,**
>
> **Being forty days tempted of the devil . . . .**
>
> **Luke 4:1,2**

> For we have not an high priest which cannot be touched with the feeling of our infirmities; but was in all points tempted like as we are, yet without sin.
>
> **Hebrews 4:15**

Thirteenth: The Holy Spirit uses visions to direct the movements of believers and to spread the Gospel:

> There was a certain man in Caesarea called Cornelius . . .
>
> He saw in a vision evidently about the ninth hour of the day an angel of God . . . [telling him]
>
> And now send men to Joppa, and call for one Simon, whose surname is Peter.
>
> **Acts 10:1,3,5**

> On the morrow, as they went on their journey, and drew nigh unto the city, Peter went up upon the housetop to pray . . . and fell into a trance . . .
>
> While Peter thought on the vision, the Spirit said unto him, Behold, three men seek thee.
>
> Arise therefore, and get thee down, and go with them, doubting nothing: for I have sent them.
>
> **Acts 10:9,10,19,20**

Note also how the Spirit used visions in the conversion of Paul:

> And there was a certain disciple at Damascus, named Ananias; and to him said the Lord in a vision, Ananias. And he said, Behold, I am here, Lord.
>
> And the Lord said unto him, Arise, and go into the street which is called Straight, and inquire in the house of Judas for one called Saul, of Tarsus: for, behold, he prayeth,
>
> And hath seen in a vision a man named Ananias coming in, and putting his hand on him, that he might receive his sight.
>
> **Acts 9:10-12**

And visions continued to be instrumental in guiding Paul during his ministry:

> **And a vision appeared to Paul in the night; There stood a man of Macedonia, and prayed him, saying, Come over into Macedonia, and help us.**
>
> **Acts 16:9**

> **Then spake the Lord to Paul in the night by a vision, Be not afraid, but speak, and hold not thy peace . . . .**
>
> **Acts 18:9**

(See also Joel 2:28-32; Acts 2:16-21.)

The Bible speaks of several kinds of visions.

1. Night visions or dreams

> **Then was the secret revealed unto Daniel in a night vision . . . .**
>
> **Daniel 2:19**

> **For God speaketh . . .**
>
> **In a dream, in a vision of the night . . . .**
>
> **Job 33:14,15**

2. Spiritual visions (when you see with your spiritual eyes)

> **And Saul arose from the earth; and when his eyes were opened, he saw no man . . . .**
>
> **Acts 9:8**

> **And Elisha prayed, and said, Lord, I pray thee, open his eyes, that he may see. And the Lord opened the eyes of the young man; and he saw: and, behold, the mountain was full of horses and chariots of fire round about Elisha.**
>
> **2 Kings 6:17**

3. Trance

> **And Balaam lifted up his eyes, and he saw . . . and the spirit of God came upon him . . .**

He hath said, which heard the words of God,
which saw the vision of the Almighty, falling into a
trance, but having his eyes open.

Numbers 24:2,4

And it came to pass, that, when I was come again
to Jerusalem, even while I prayed in the temple, I was
in a trance.

Acts 22:17

4. Open visions (when you see with your natural
eyes)

And the angel of the Lord spake unto Philip,
saying, Arise, and go toward the south, unto the way
that goeth down from Jerusalem unto Gaza, which is
desert.

Acts 8:26

Where there is no vision, the people perish . . . .
Proverbs 29:18

The Bible encourages all believers to grow into the
maturity of dreams and revelations:

Paul says, . . . I will come to visions and
revelations . . . (2 Cor. 12:1).

And the promise of the Holy Spirit brings this
encouragement:

And it shall come to pass in the last days, saith
God, I will pour out my Spirit upon all flesh: and your
sons and your daughters shall prophesy, and your
young men shall see visions, and your old men shall
dream dreams.

Acts 2:17

Fourteenth: The Holy Spirit directs in the selection
of spiritual leaders and gospel workers:

As they ministered to the Lord, and fasted, the
Holy Ghost said, Separate me Barnabas and Saul for
the work whereunto I have called them.

Acts 13:2

Fifteenth: The Holy Spirit gives wisdom in establishing standards of conduct:

> For it seemed good to the Holy Ghost, and to us, to lay upon you no greater burden than these necessary things.
>
> Acts 15:28

Sixteenth: Prayer is effective as the Holy Spirit helps believers intercede:

> Likewise the Spirit also helpeth our infirmities: for we know not what we should pray for as we ought: but the Spirit itself [Himself] maketh intercession for us with groanings which cannot be uttered.
>
> And he that searcheth the hearts knoweth what is the mind of the Spirit, because he maketh intercession for the saints according to the will of God.
>
> Romans 8:26,27

(See also 1 John 5:14,15, where every prayer that is prayed in the *will of God* is answered!)

> But ye, beloved, building up yourselves on your most holy faith, praying in the Holy Ghost,
>
> Keep yourselves in the love of God . . . .
>
> Jude 20,21

Seventeenth: When it seems the enemy will win, the Holy Spirit lifts up a standard against him:

> . . . When the enemy shall come in like a flood, the spirit of the Lord shall lift up a standard against him.
>
> Isaiah 59:19

> For the eyes of the Lord run to and fro throughout the whole earth, to shew himself strong in the behalf of them whose heart is perfect toward him.
>
> 2 Chronicles 16:9

Eighteenth: The Holy Spirit speaks to others through believers' lips, both in their own tongue and in various heavenly languages (tongues):

> For it is not ye that speak, but the Spirit of your Father which speaketh in you.
>
> Matthew 10:20

> And they were all filled with the Holy Ghost, and began to speak with other tongues, as the Spirit gave them utterance.
>
> Acts 2:4

(See also Acts 10:44-49; 19:1-6; 1 Cor. 12:1; 14:40.)

Nineteenth: Sometimes the Holy Spirit will forbid good activity because it is not God's timing:

> Now when they had gone throughout Phrygia and the region of Galatia, and were forbidden of the Holy Ghost to preach the word in Asia,

> After they were come to Mysia, they assayed to go into Bithynia: but the Spirit suffered them not.
>
> Acts 16:6,7

Twentieth: The Holy Spirit always leads into the right way of truth:

> Howbeit when he, the Spirit of truth, is come, he will guide you into all truth: for he shall not speak of himself: but whatsoever he shall hear, that shall he speak: and he will shew you things to come.

> He shall glorify me [Jesus]: for he shall receive of mine, and shall shew it unto you.
>
> John 16:13,14

The Bible tells how the Holy Spirit manifested Himself in many other ways. Yet, these twenty examples are given as a cross-section to encourage you not to limit His wonder-working power to any pre-conceived ideas you might already have developed. Realize that His power is promised to *every* believer who will follow after truth and seek to live and act according to the purposes and plans of God.

Remember, too, that the days immediately following the resurrection of Christ are the purest examples we can have of the Holy Spirit at work in the lives of believers. This is *your* pattern. When men compiled the inspired books of the Bible, they called this section "the Acts of the Apostles." Though the book itself is inspired, the title that man gave might best be called *"the Acts of the Holy Spirit."*

The Holy Spirit has never been taken from the world. He is still at work, revealing Christ in the power of His Resurrection. Jesus said, **And I, if I be lifted up . . . will draw all men unto me** (John 12:32). There is no "amen" at the end of the book of Acts, which would have indicated that the work of the Holy Spirit was for those ancient times and not for today. In God's eyes, the account of the Holy Spirit and His ministry to the Church is still being written through the lives and witness of Jesus' followers — *you* and *me!*

Today, we should surrender ourselves completely to Christ as Paul did, when he said:

> **I am crucified with Christ: nevertheless I live; yet not I, but Christ liveth in me: and the life which I now live in the flesh I live by the faith of the Son of God, who loved me, and gave himself for me.**
> **Galatians 2:20**

Paul's desire was not *just* to know God's will but to *do* God's will and to live his life in a way that would please his Lord daily. As the Spirit of God directed Paul's life daily, He will direct our lives as we desire to fulfill God's will in our daily walk with Him. We will know the Father's voice, and the Holy Spirit will lead us into all truth.

Remember this: God's will will not lead you where His grace cannot keep you!

———————

———————

"As a Spirit-filled believer, see the importance of your prayer language. When faith is weak and your understanding is unfruitful, that's when the Holy Spirit gives an extra boost to your weak transmission."

———————

———————

10

Seven Guidelines for Your Spirit-Led Walk

In previous chapters, I have discussed the various facets of spiritual guidance, the Spirit-filled believer's position in Christ, and touched on some of the obstacles which believers must overcome. This final chapter presents some specific guidelines for your Spirit-led walk.

I suggest that you read these seven points prayerfully with a firm determination to make them a daily habit. Then, after you have finished this chapter, go back through the entire book and read it again, especially the points which relate to your individual needs.

First: Each day, know the joy of hearing God's voice through the Word.

Jesus said:

> **These things have I spoken unto you, that my joy might remain in you, and that *your joy might be full*.**
> **John 15:11**

John said:

> **And these things write we unto you, that *your joy may be full*.**
>
> **1 John 1:4**

According to these verses, the highest kind of joy, the *full* joy, is that which springs from God's Word. To be fully victorious in life, you must become familiar with God's Word and make it your rule of life.

Acquaint yourself with the books of the Bible and their location. Commit select portions of the Scriptures to memory, that you may use them to witness to others *and* for instant recall in times of personal crisis and need. When doubts come and you face adversity, begin to quote God's promises which the Holy Spirit will quicken in your heart. You will discover this to be a real source of victory, bringing rich seasons of uplift and refreshing joy.

In the book of Joshua, God commands us saying,

> **This book of the law shall not depart out of thy mouth; but thou shalt meditate therein day and night, that thou mayest observe to do according to all that is written therein: for then thou shalt make thy way prosperous, and then thou shalt have good success.**
> **Joshua 1:8**

We are admonished by Paul to:

> **Put on the whole armour of God . . .**

> **Above all, taking the shield of faith, wherewith ye shall be able to quench all the fiery darts of the wicked.**

> **And take the helmet of salvation, and the sword of the Spirit, which is the word of God.**
> **Ephesians 6:11,16,17**

There are many other Scriptures, relative to the Word and its rightful place in the Christian life, throughout this book. Read these Scriptures again and consider them in the context where they appear. Through them, you will gain strong faith and confidence in God.

Second: Each day, know the joy of talking to God in prayer.

Jesus said:

> **Verily, verily, I say unto you, whatsoever ye shall ask the Father in my name, he will give it you . . . ask, and ye shall receive, that your joy may be full.**
> **John 16:23,24**

> **If ye abide in me, and my words abide in you, ye shall ask what ye will, and it shall be done unto you.**
> **John 15:7**

As God pointed out in the verses above, when you read God's Word, it is *God talking to you;* on the other hand, when you pray, it is *you talking to God.* So be diligent and continue to read the Word and pray, understanding that in this manner, you will continue to nurture, and be nourished by, this two-way communication between you and the Father.

To help you to remember these vital points, let's use the illustration of a CB radio, transmitting and receiving signals. You know the popular phrase of CBers, "10-4," or "That's right on." Well, here are two "10-4s" for you to act on, by which you will be saying, "That's right on" to God's promises:

> **And when he putteth forth his own sheep, he goeth before them, and the sheep follow him:** *for they know his voice.*
> **John 10:4**

You know His voice through the Word.

> . . . **Thy prayers and thine alms are come up for a memorial before God.**
>
> **Acts 10:4**

God always registers the petition of faith in heaven, and has promised to *answer.*

Sometimes you may feel that your transmission is weak and your signals are not breaking through to the throne. In such times, hold fast to God's promises:

> **He shall call upon me, and *I will answer him:* I will be with him in trouble; I will deliver him, and honour him.**
>
> **Psalm 91:15**

> **And this is the confidence that we have in him, that, if we ask any thing according to his will, *he heareth us:***

> **And if we know that he hear us, whatsoever we ask, we know that we have the petitions that we desired of him.**
>
> **1 John 5:14,15**

As a Spirit-filled believer, you must see the importance of your prayer language. When faith is weak and your understanding is unfruitful, that's when the Holy Spirit gives an extra boost to your weak transmission. Have confidence in His ability to get through to the Father and allow the Spirit to intercede for you:

> **For if I pray in an unknown tongue, my spirit prayeth, but my understanding is unfruitful.**
>
> **I Corinthians 14:14**

> **But ye, beloved, building up yourselves on your most holy faith, praying in the Holy Ghost.**
>
> **Jude 20**

As you pray, believe that God's receiver is strong enough to pick up your signal. He is constantly searching the wave lengths and *your call will get through as you pray in the Spirit.*

> Likewise the Spirit also helpeth our infirmities: for we know not what we should pray for as we ought: but the Spirit itself maketh intercession for us with groanings which cannot be uttered.
>
> And he that searcheth the hearts knoweth what is the mind of the Spirit, because he maketh intercession for the saints according to the will of God.
>
> **Romans 8:26,27**

Third: Each day, know the joy of sharing Christ with others.

Allowing God to *talk to you* through His Word and *talking to Him* through prayer is vital to our Christian walk, but so is *talking to others about God* through our Christian witness.

This may sound strange to you, but I say it on the basis of the Scriptures: there is no richer joy on earth, nor is there any higher joy in heaven, than that of winning souls to Christ:

> I say unto you, that likewise joy shall be in heaven over one sinner that repenteth, more than over ninety and nine just persons, which need no repentance.
>
> Likewise, I say unto you, there is joy in the presence of the angels of God over one sinner that repenteth.
>
> **Luke 15:7,10**

If heaven's hosts take time from their heavenly duties to rejoice over sinners coming to Christ, then the joy of soulwinning must somehow exceed all other joys. How much more should this challenge you and me to make evangelism our aim in life? Since there is rejoicing in heaven over souls coming to Christ, we should pray all the more: **Thy kingdom come. Thy will be done in earth, as it is in heaven** (Matt. 6:10). For God is **. . . not willing that any should perish, but that all should come to repentance** (2 Pet. 3:9). Psalm 126:6 says, **He that goeth forth and weepeth, bearing precious seed, shall doubtless come again with rejoicing, bringing his sheaves with him.**

Fourth: Associate with other Spirit-filled believers.

The Bible says:

> **Not forsaking the assembling of ourselves together, as the manner of some is; but exhorting one another: and so much the more, as ye see the day approaching.**
> **Hebrews 10:25**

> **But if we walk in the light, as he is in the light, we have fellowship one with another, and the blood of Jesus Christ his Son cleanseth us from all sin.**
> **1 John 1:7**

Let the example of the early-day believers who **continued steadfastly in the apostles' doctrine and fellowship, and in breaking of bread, and in prayers** (Acts 2:42) be your guide.

It's been said that water will never rise above its source. Remember too, that your Christian experience and your walk with Christ can never be higher than the source from which you draw. Therefore, to learn more about knowing the Father's voice, associate with those believers and Christian leaders who believe that He speaks today. Be cautious of those who believe and teach otherwise. If you wanted to learn about reaping a harvest, you would go to a farmer who planted seeds and cultivated his crops. If you want to learn more about the Spirit-filled life, about God's miracles and the gifts of the Spirit, don't go to those who believe and teach that these experiences are not for today. Rather, surround yourself with Bible-believing people, that they may be . . . **comforted together with you by the mutual faith** . . . (Rom. 1:12) that you have in Christ. We would do well if we followed the advice given to us in Proverbs 13:20 which says, **He that walketh with wise men shall be wise: but a companion of fools shall be destroyed.**

Fifth: Submit yourself to spiritual leaders.

> **Obey them that have the rule over you, and submit yourselves: for they watch for your souls, as they that must give account, that they may do it with joy . . . .**
> **Hebrews 13:17**

> **Likewise, ye younger, submit yourselves unto the elder. Yea, all of you be subject one to another, and be clothed with humility: for God resisteth the proud, but giveth grace to the humble.**
> **1 Peter 5:5**

Remember that God has set pastors, evangelists and teachers as ministry gifts in the church for your ministry, in order to bring you to the position Christ has in mind for you. These leaders are . . .

> **For the perfecting of the saints, for the work of the ministry, for the edifying of the body of Christ:**
> [That we] . . . **may grow up into him in all things, which is the head, even Christ.**
> **Ephesians 4:12,15**

Sixth: Live a righteous life, in the fear of God.

To be *righteous* simply means to live in *right* standing with Him, walking in the light of the

Scriptures to do what is *right* in His eyes. You can only do this as you follow the example of Christ and seek to carry out His mission on earth. As you take this position in faith, God looks upon your life through Christ and declares you to be *righteous*. Please understand there is a difference between enjoying having been made *righteous in Christ* and *self-righteousness*.

Romans 4:3 says, **Abraham believed God, and it was counted unto him for righteousness.** Abraham accepted God's Word, embraced it as his rule of life and submitted himself to its control. As a result, God accepted him as a *friend*, who fulfilled all of His requirements:

> **And the scripture was fulfilled which saith, Abraham believed God, and it was imputed unto him for righteousness: and he was called the Friend of God.**
>
> **James 2:23**

Jesus said, "You are my friends" in John 15:15. But remember, . . . **whosoever therefore will be a friend of the world is the enemy of God** (James 4:4).

> **For the grace of God that bringeth salvation hath appeared to all men,**
>
> **Teaching us that, denying ungodliness and worldly lusts, we should live soberly, righteously, and godly, in this present world.**
>
> **Titus 2:11,12**

Seventh: Live in expectancy of Christ's return.

> **Looking for that blessed hope, and the glorious appearing of the great God and our Savior Jesus Christ;**

> Who gave himself for us, that he might redeem us from all iniquity, and purify unto himself a peculiar people, zealous of good works.
>
> **Titus 2:13,14**

> And every man that hath this hope in him purifieth himself, even as he is pure.
>
> **1 John 3:3**

> Therefore be ye also ready: for in such an hour as ye think not the Son of man cometh.
>
> **Matthew 24:44**

There is one final Scripture that I will use with an illustration on knowing the Father's voice.

> And the very God of peace sanctify you wholly; and I pray God your whole spirit and soul and body be preserved blameless unto the coming of our Lord Jesus Christ.
>
> **1 Thessalonians 5:23**

This Scripture doesn't say you will be kept *faultless*. Many people fail to recognize the difference between being *faultless* and being *blameless*. In their failure to see this distinction, they become subject to all sorts of guilt complexes and self-condemnation. Let me explain.

Suppose you are the father of a small son who is just learning to walk. You beckon to him from across the room to walk to you. The little toddler pulls himself up beside a chair, wobbles on his legs that haven't yet gained sufficient strength to fully support his body and plops to the floor. Again he pulls himself up, takes an uncertain step toward you and falls. Immediately he gets up and takes two steps. He grins happily at his great success just before his legs collapse beneath him for a third time.

As an intelligent observer, you certainly can't say that your child's walk is *faultless*. But to you as a parent, his courageous attempt to walk is entirely *blameless* for he is doing all he possibly can to respond to his father's voice.

That is basically why I have written this book. I see so many Christians who, like the toddler, try to respond to their Father's voice and fall short. Because of their lack of teaching, they allow themselves to become discouraged, and many give up altogether.

To these people, I want to say: *try again! You have your faults, but your Father holds you blameless as long as you keep on trying. So try again, and again: you are becoming stronger each time you try. Thank God, you are learning to know and respond to your Father's voice!*

Dr. Bill Basansky, born in the Soviet Union, was confined in Nazi prison camps during World War II. The gripping story of how God miraculously delivered him and brought him to America after the war is told in his first book, called *Escape From Terror*.

After serving in the U.S. Air Force for four years, Bill worked as a police officer in California and went to college to receive his teaching degree. After receiving this degree, he taught in a public school. During this time, he became addicted to alcohol and drugs while trying to relieve the constant pain he suffered in his back from an injury received while in the Air Force. In 1969, this back ailment caused paralysis in his legs, and Bill contemplated suicide. In desperation, he cried out for help. God marvelously healed him and delivered him instantly from eight years of alcohol and drug addiction. He accepted Jesus Christ as his Lord and Savior, and soon after, received the Baptism of the Holy Spirit.

For five years, Bill was a professor at Oral Roberts University in Tulsa, Oklahoma. He received his master's degree from the University of Oklahoma and his Ph.D. from Union University in California. Dr. Basansky resided in Tulsa, with his wife and family, while he ministered extensively throughout America and Canada through Bill Basansky Ministries.

Bill has authored many books which are reaching those who have not accepted Jesus as Lord and teaching the Body of Christ how to live victoriously.

As a man sent from God, Bill has ministered God's healing Word to America. He has sought to bring hope, healing and faith where darkness and despair have prevailed. His teachings on the Christian family, his personal counseling sessions and his crusades have had a vital impact throughout North America.

The miraculous power of God is manifested in Bill Basansky's meetings. Wherever he ministers, God confirms His Word, performing many outstanding miracles. He has been a guest on PTL and CBN. His television program, *Rise and Be Healed*, has stirred the faith of multitudes. Dr. Basansky was a guest speaker for the 1984 "Day of Prayer" Celebration and "The Constitutional Liberties Rally" in Washington, D.C. He is also involved in the "Healing of the Nation" ministry.

In fulfilling the call of God on their ministry, Dr. Basansky and his wife, Bea, moved the ministry headquarters from Tulsa to Fort Myers, Florida, to found *Love and Grace Fellowship* there.

To contact the author, write: Bill Basansky
Love and Grace Fellowship • P. O. Box 7126
Fort Myers, Florida 33911

Additional copies are available at your local bookstore
or by writing:

Harrison House
P. O. Box 35035 • Tulsa, OK 74153

In Canada contact: • Word Alive • P. O. Box 284
Niverville, Manitoba • CANADA R0A 1E0